£20

THE
SEVERN & WYE
RAILWAY

AN ILLUSTRATED HISTORY OF

THE
SEVERN & WYE
RAILWAY

VOLUME ONE

BY

IAN POPE, BOB HOW AND PAUL KARAU

WILD SWAN PUBLICATIONS LTD.

FOR
'DEAN FORESTER'
Harry Paar, Peter Copeland & Rev. David Tipper

Designed by Paul Karau
Typesetting by Berkshire Publishing Services
Photo reproduction and offset plates by Oxford Litho Plates Ltd.
Printed in Oxford

Published by
WILD SWAN PUBLICATIONS LTD.,
Hopgoods Farm Cottage, Upper Bucklebury, Berks.

CONTENTS

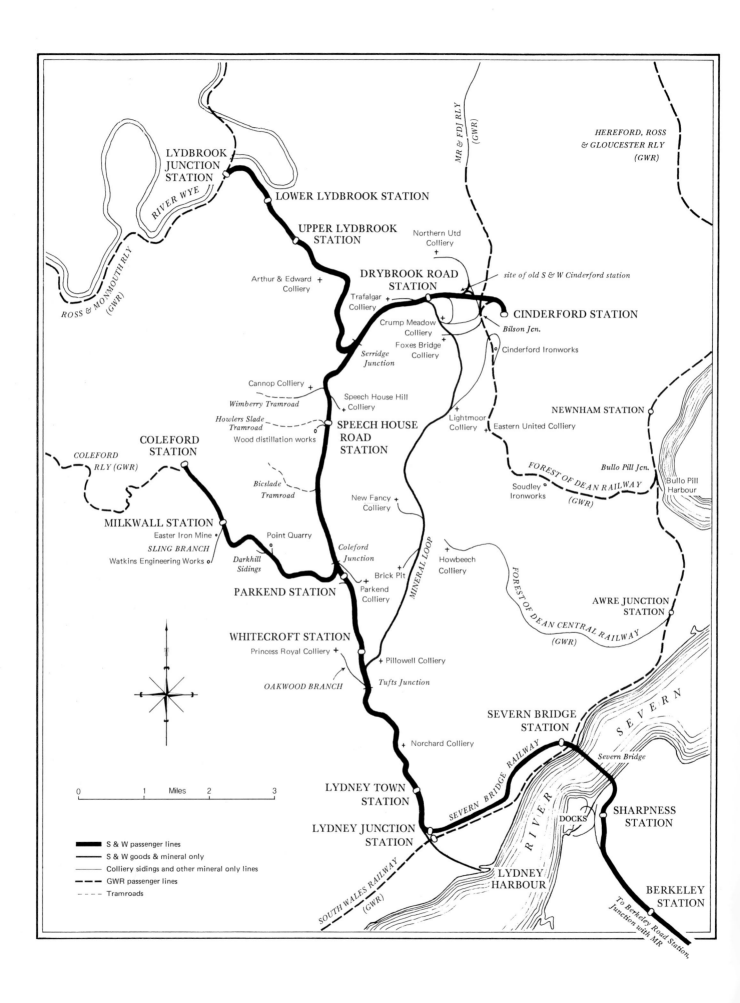

LYDBROOK JUNCTION STATION

LOWER LYDBROOK STATION

UPPER LYDBROOK STATION

RIVER WYE

ROSS & MONMOUTH RLY (GWR)

MR & FDJ RLY (GWR)

HEREFORD, ROSS & GLOUCESTER RLY (GWR)

Northern Utd Colliery

Arthur & Edward Colliery

DRYBROOK ROAD STATION

site of old S & W Cinderford station

Trafalgar Colliery

CINDERFORD STATION

Crump Meadow Colliery

Bilson Jcn.

Serridge Junction

Foxes Bridge Colliery

Cinderford Ironworks

Cannop Colliery

Speech House Hill Colliery

Lightmoor Colliery

Wimberry Tramroad

NEWNHAM STATION

Howlers Slade Tramroad

SPEECH HOUSE ROAD STATION

Eastern United Colliery

Wood distillation works

COLEFORD STATION

COLEFORD RLY (GWR)

Bullo Pill Jcn.

Bicslade Tramroad

Soudley Ironworks

FOREST OF DEAN RAILWAY (GWR)

Bullo Pill Harbour

New Fancy Colliery

MILKWALL STATION

Easter Iron Mine

Point Quarry

SLING BRANCH

Watkins Engineering Works

Darkhill Sidings

Coleford Junction

Howbeech Colliery

MINERAL LOOP

FOREST OF DEAN CENTRAL RAILWAY (GWR)

Brick Pit

PARKEND STATION

Parkend Colliery

AWRE JUNCTION STATION

WHITECROFT STATION

Princess Royal Colliery

Pillowell Colliery

OAKWOOD BRANCH

Tufts Junction

SEVERN BRIDGE STATION

SEVERN

Norchard Colliery

Severn Bridge

SHARPNESS STATION

LYDNEY TOWN STATION

SEVERN BRIDGE RAILWAY

DOCKS

RIVER SEVERN

LYDNEY JUNCTION STATION

LYDNEY HARBOUR

BERKELEY STATION

SOUTH WALES RAILWAY (GWR)

To Berkeley Road Station, Junction with MR

0   1   Miles   2   3

——— S & W passenger lines
——— S & W goods & mineral only
——— Colliery sidings and other mineral only lines
- - - GWR passenger lines
- - - Tramroads

INTRODUCTION

THE Forest of Dean lies in the County of Gloucestershire between the Rivers Severn and Wye. The size of its area has varied much over the centuries but it was based on the Hundred of Saint Briavels. In ancient days it was a wild and impenetrable area settled by a tribe of Britons known as the Silures who may have worked the mineral wealth under the Forest. Certainly the iron-ore was being worked by the Romans who eventually settled the Forest. From the time of the Domesday Book the area was a royal hunting ground and came to belong to the Crown, as it does to this day.

Geologically the Forest is a basin of carboniferous rocks containing both iron-bearing rocks around the edge and coal measures in the centre. The basin has a length of approximately twelve miles and a width of about eight.

The right of working the minerals and stone within the Forest has been for centuries past, and still is, vested in all male persons of the age of 21 years who have worked for a year and a day in a coal or iron mine and who were born within the boundaries of the Hundred of Saint Briavels. Upon proof of these requirements he may be registered as a 'Free Miner' by the Gaveller who is the representative of the Crown within the Forest. The Forest itself was originally administered by the Surveyor General of Woods and Forests, and after 1810 by the Commissioners of Woods, Forests and Land Revenues of the Crown, until the formation of the Forestry Commission in 1919. All land taken for industrial purposes was leased from the Crown on 'licences'.

The mineral deposits within the Forest are divided into tracts called 'gales'. The areas, and owners, of these were defined in a survey following the 1838 Dean Forest Mines Act conducted by Thomas Sopwith, John Probyn and John Buddle which led to the 1841 award of coal and iron mines. Prior to this, minerals had been worked in a haphazard manner and many disputes arose between adjoining miners. There are, however, several areas called 'exempted lands', as they are under private ownership, such as the Lydney Park Estate of the Bathurst family. A gale can only be granted to a Free Miner who then pays an annual rent, 'dead rent', and a royalty on tonnage raised, to the Crown. When a Free Miner is granted a gale he is called the 'galee'. He can then either work the minerals himself or sell, transfer, assign or dispose of the gale to others, but any such sale or assignment must be recorded by the Gaveller. These arrangements enabled individuals other than Free Miners to acquire mining rights, thereby allowing companies with capital from outside the Forest to exploit a gale.

A gale may comprise one or more seams of coal and two or more gales may lie vertically over one another but belong to different galees. The lower seams of coal were known as the 'deep gales' and, until the start of the 20th century, were little exploited due to the depth at which the coal lay beneath the surface and the small size of the area covered by the gale. In 1904, to overcome this problem, a further Dean Forest Mines Act was passed empowering the Gaveller to amalgamate certain gales to form a larger area and therefore make the working of the deep gales an economic proposition.

The coal measures within the Forest basin can be divided into three main groups according to depth. The uppermost group is the Supra-Pennant, followed by the Pennant, whilst the deepest measures are the Trenchard group which contains the most valuable coal seam within the coalfield — the Coleford High Delf. It was this seam which required the 1904 amalgamation in order for it to be worked profitably. The total thickness of coal measures is about 2,300 feet, comprising 22 seams with a total thickness of 35 feet of coal. In practice twelve of these seams have sufficient thickness of coal to be workable.

The Coleford High Delf seam has an average thickness of 4 ft although it reaches 7-8 ft in areas of the coalfield.

The iron-bearing rocks which underlie the coal measures and outcrop around the outside of the coal seams on the north, west and east sides, can be divided into three regions. These are the eastern, which runs from Wigpool to Soudley through Cinderford, the north-western running from Drybrook to Staunton, and the south-western running from Staunton to Lydney. Of these areas the eastern was the most productive, yielding over 3 million tons between 1842 and 1899. The iron mines here, notably the Shakemantle and Buckshaft mines at Ruspidge, were the deepest in the Forest but suffered heavily from problems with water, and it was this, together with the drop in demand for iron-ore, which led to their closure before the end of the nineteenth century.

The north-western district proved to have virtually no reserves of ore. Several levels were driven in the Lydbrook area but ore was not proved in sufficient quantities to make working them profitable. The south-western area, however, was quite productive; here the ore was mainly won around the Coleford and Milkwall areas by deep mining and it was near Milkwall that the last iron ore was worked in the Forest on a regular basis until the 1920s with a brief revival during the Second World War.

With the abundance of iron ore plus the surrounding timber to make charcoal, iron furnaces were established in the Forest. Iron was smelted here during Roman times, and possibly earlier, and from then on small furnaces were set up on many sites. Improved techniques in iron smelting and the use of coke rather than charcoal, led to the building of larger furnaces, notably those at Cinderford, Soudley and Parkend, but again, due to trade depression and foreign competition, all had closed by the end of the nineteenth century.

Various industries grew up within the Forest as a result of the iron and coal mining. The production of charcoal for the iron furnaces later led to the setting up of chemical works, whilst colour and ochre works were a direct result

1

of iron mining. Engineering works were established to serve the requirements of the mines and several brick-works were set up to supply the demand for building materials, and to utilize the clay removed during mining and quarrying operations.

It was at the start of the nineteenth century that the industrialization of the Forest really began. Before this time the Free Miners worked small areas and there were many scores of small concerns working the minerals close to the surface. There was a lack of capital to exploit the mineral wealth within the Forest and it took outsiders to bring the financial backing, but the Foresters were very wary of people from outside coming into the area and taking away their livelihood. Soon, however, outsiders did move in and expanded the coal mines and re-opened moribund iron works, but they were hampered by the lack of communications within the area.

At the end of the eighteenth century the Forest was still a virtually impenetrable area; its roads, such as they

were, were virtually impassable in winter, and pack animals were the order of the day. Minerals from the Forest therefore cost so much to move to the rivers for shipment that by the time they reached the markets the price was uncompetitive. There existed then a need for an efficient means of transport within the Forest and again it took outside capital to provide it. The answer was a network of tramroads using the horse as motive power. Three main tramroads were built between 1809 and 1815, the Bullo Pill Railway Company which served the eastern side of the Forest from the area north of Cinderford down to the River Severn at Bullo Pill, the Monmouth Railway Company which linked Monmouth with Coleford, and the Severn and Wye Railway and Canal Company, the largest of the three, which linked the rivers of its name between Lydney and Lydbrook, thereby serving the western side of the Forest. It is the last mentioned which is the subject of the first volume of this series.

SIMPLIFIED GEOLOGICAL DIAGRAM

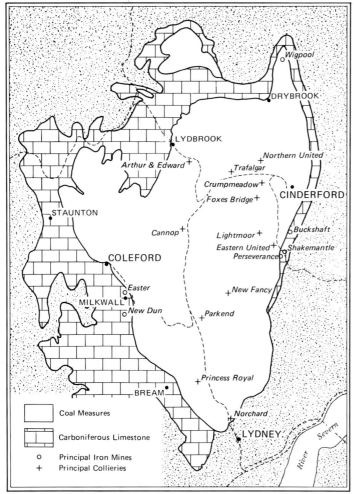

After F. M. Trotter; Geology of the Forest of Dean Coal
and Iron-ore Field, H.M.S.O. 1942.

Section through the coal measures showing the arrangement of the main seams.

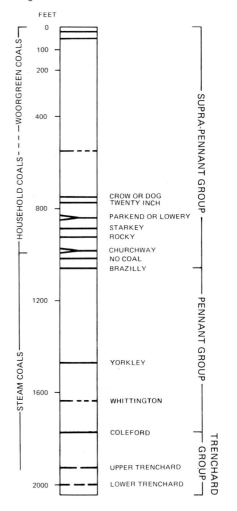

CHAPTER ONE

TRAMROAD DAYS

ALTHOUGH the tramroads are outside the intended scope of this book, it is necessary to outline their development in brief in order to establish the very foundations on which the Severn & Wye Railway was later built. In fact, the concept of a tramroad linking the Rivers Severn and Wye was first raised in 1799 by men of Hereford and Gloucester, in search of cheaper coal. Several schemes were proposed during the years that followed before the 'Lydney and Lydbrook Railway' was secured by an Act of Parliament on 10th June 1809. The Act authorized the construction of a line between the two places named, together with eight branches, and gave three years for the completion of the majority of the work. In June the following year a second Act was obtained which altered the title of the concern to 'The Severn and Wye Railway and Canal Company' and also sanctioned the construction of a harbour and canal at Lydney.

Contracts for the construction of the line were let in August 1809 to several contractors whose work was overseen by the Company's engineer, Astley Bowdler. He had been appointed in June at a salary of £210 per annum, for which he also held the office of clerk. After a year, however, he specialized as engineer, taking a corresponding drop in pay to £100, whilst Morgan Parry was appointed clerk and manager for 200 guineas a year. Bowdler, however, fell out with the committee of management and was dismissed in August 1810 and replaced by a Josias Jessop, who in turn was replaced in July 1811 by Thomas Sheasby, who served the company well until his retirement in 1847.

The permanent way consisted of L-section cast iron plates, 3 feet in length and weighing 42 lbs, spiked to stone blocks with iron nails. The area between the two lines of plates was filled and levelled with gravel or furnace cinders. Originally the gauge was 3′ 6″ but as the years went by this gradually widened!

Traffic on the line commenced in June 1810 but was soon temporarily halted as goods were being carried virtually free of charge. This was due to the fact that no weighing machines had been erected. The Severn & Wye gained its revenue from collecting tolls for the use of its line, rates being fixed for different commodities and charged for by weight and distance carried. The company itself was not a carrier and apparently owned no vehicles, traders wishing to use the line having to provide their own wagons and horses.

The original Act had authorized a capital of £35,000, mainly in £50 shares, together with an extra £20,000 if needed, but the majority of this had been used up by the middle of 1811 and another Act was gained to sanction an increase in capital of £35,000. However, by this time the company was already in financial difficulties as Lydney harbour was only partially complete and there was still no seaborne outlet. Disputes were also arising within the company as quite a few of the proprietors had industrial interests within the Forest and each, therefore, wanted the branch which would best serve his interests completed first.

At a special meeting of the management committee, in March 1813, it was announced that, although water had been let into the canal and basin, the concern was in debt to the sum of £10,000, and the following month a writ was issued against the company in respect of £7,000 owed on tramplates.

The financial position was again eased in May 1814 with the passing of yet another Act, the fourth, which increased the capital by another £30,000, although it appears not to have made any lasting difference as in 1816 employees were informed that their wages would be lowered.

As well as struggling with the constant shortage of money, the threat of competition also hung over the Severn & Wye for the greater part of its life. During the 1820s the company spent considerable sums in fighting off the threat posed by projected new lines within the Forest, some £600, for instance, being spent against the Purton Pill Steam Carriage Road which was intended to serve the central area of the Forest. In 1839 a proposal by the Forest of Dean Railway to construct a new harbour and a line to serve its tramroad in the eastern valleys was fiercely contested by the S & W and eventually dropped.

During the 1820s and '30s the Severn & Wye continued to operate its tramroad system carrying ever increasing traffic, but, as the company went into the next decade, it came under pressure to modernize its line. The effects of the 1838 Dean Forest Mines Act were now being felt in that, with the clear definition of areas, works were being modernized and extended with a corresponding need for improved transport facilities. Further pressure came from the South Wales Railway Company who, in 1846, were applying to extend their line from Chepstow to Gloucester. They wanted to purchase the neighbouring Forest of Dean tramroad and build a line alongside the Severn & Wye from Lydney to Churchway. The Severn & Wye attempted to sell out to them but the two companies could not agree on a price. A Commons committee then proposed that the purchase of the Severn & Wye should be included in the Bill, to which the South Wales Co. objected.

In 1847 a further South Wales Bill was before Parliament to authorize the conversion of the Forest of Dean tramroad to an edge railway. The Severn & Wye vigorously opposed this as being injurious to their trade, but the South Wales company gained their Act after a clause had been inserted giving the Severn & Wye £15,000 to assist the conversion to broad gauge.

Also in 1847 Thomas Sheasby, who had been manager, secretary and engineer, retired, but remained a consulting engineer to the company. He was succeeded as clerk by George Baker Keeling, who later also became secretary. Another consulting engineer at this time was Thomas Blackwell of Bristol, whose assistant in 1854 was G. B. Keeling's son, George William, who also came to work on the Severn & Wye.

The South Wales line was opened in September 1851 and traffic interchange facilities were constructed at Lydney, highlighting the great disparity between the two modes of transport. In the same year, Blackwell commenced a survey of the Severn & Wye with a view to improving the system, while yet another threat was being proposed under the name of the Forest of Dean Central Railway, a direct descendant of the Purton Pill Steam Carriage Road proposals. Again the Severn & Wye fiercely opposed it.

Blackwell's proposals, completed in 1852, included a scheme to convert the Severn & Wye to a single line of broad gauge. His ideas were submitted to the Commissioners of Woods who, in their reply in May 1852, required the S & W to meet various conditions before they would grant their approval. One of these was that a central line should be built into the Forest independently of the Severn & Wye who were to offer no objection. The Severn & Wye took great exception to this and negotiations with the Commissioners ceased.

It was then decided by the company that, rather than convert to a railway, they would improve their existing line, complete various proposed extensions, improve the harbour and become carriers themselves using locomotives. The cost of this was estimated at £68,000 plus £14,000 of the South Wales Railway money which as yet was untouched. The scheme was submitted to Parliament and sanctioned in August 1853. However, the use of locomotives was not in fact implemented until 1864 as their successful use on the tramplates was in doubt.

The Severn & Wye thus proceeded at a very steady pace throughout the 1850s and '60s. In March 1857 G. W. Keeling, at the age of 18, was appointed inspector of works, becoming engineer in 1860 and ordering the first locomotive to be used on the tramroad. This was an 0—4—0 well tank built by Messrs. Fletcher Jennings of Whitehaven and delivered to Lydney in October 1864. It was followed by three similar locomotives the following year. The fifth and last of the tramway locomotives was delivered in November 1865 and was also built by Fletcher's, but as an 0—6—0 designed for use on the heavily graded Moseley Green branch.

In March 1866 an anonymous offer was made to purchase the Severn & Wye but nothing came of this. Pressure was, however, again mounting at this time for the company to improve its line and facilities.

A scene typical of the later years on the surviving horse-drawn tramroads. Its equine motive power keeping strictly to the clear path within the plateway, a load of stone slabs descends the Bicslade branch in June 1938 from Bixhead Quarry to the stone works alongside the transhipment wharf on the Severn & Wye main line north of Coleford Junction.   *B. Baxter*

CHAPTER TWO

THE SEVERN & WYE ON EDGE RAIL
1868-94

BY 1867 the Directors had become aware, rather belatedly, that the tramroad was no longer adequate to keep up with the increasing traffic. The traders who used the tramroad had long been pressing for the conversion to edge rail, particularly as the Severn & Wye's neighbours, the Great Western's Forest of Dean branch and the Forest of Dean Central Railway (which was just about to open) were both laid with it, and problems were caused by the need to tranship loads onto the broad gauge South Wales Railway at Lydney.

At a Directors' meeting in May 1867, therefore, it was decided to provide broad gauge railway accommodation from Lydney to Parkend and thence to Wimberry Junction. Keeling put forward an estimate of £95,298 for the conversion, which included the cost of a line to Lydbrook and an extension of the Moseley Green branch to Foxes Bridge. However, as always with the Severn & Wye, economy was the watchword and by November it was just the conversion of the line to Wimberry that was laid before the Directors at an estimated £33,000.

The company first approached the Commissioners of Woods for financial assistance, but when they received no help from this quarter they secured a Board of Trade certificate, in 1868, to raise £38,000 extra capital. Tenders were sought for permanent way materials and in January 1868 an offer of 75¾ lb per yard edge rail at £5 per ton was accepted from J. W. Armstrong of Carmarthen, who at this time was the Hereford Divisional Engineer of the Great Western Railway, and broad gauge sleepers were supplied by Messrs. T. B. & S. Batchelor of Cardiff at 3/8d. each. It was also decided at the same time that the six-wheeled tramroad locomotive No. 5 should be converted to broad gauge at an estimated cost of £200.

In March 1868 six hundred tons of edge rail were delivered to Lydney at a cost of some £3,000 and in May the Directors ordered a new broad gauge locomotive from Messrs. Fletcher Jennings. In September it was reported that the conversion of No. 5, which was carried out at Lydney, was nearly complete and that the broad gauge line from Lydney to Wimberry would be ready in about two or three weeks. The broad gauge was laid alongside the tramroad, mainly on the east side, as this avoided having level crossings with the tramroad, most of its branches running off to the west. Traders were informed that the line would be ready for traffic at the end of September, but this was not to be.

On 11th November the Directors took a trip up the new line behind No. 5, now named *Forester*, and on 27th November the new locomotive was delivered to Lydney by sea. The company may have been looking to the future for once as this locomotive was a 'convertible' which allowed for the impending change to standard gauge. It was an 0-6-0 side tank named *Robin Hood*.

Permission for traffic operation on the broad gauge, however, was refused by the Commissioners of Woods until a sharp curve near Whitecroft had been avoided. This would have involved a deviation of about 200 yards but, although a short length of embankment was actually constructed for the deviation (and can still be seen today) it was not completed. The reason for this is not apparent and the original course was maintained. The first traffic, which included some Welsh coke going to the ironworks at Parkend, was not carried until 19th April 1869. Traffic was initially slow to appear, mainly due to the fact that the traders had not arranged to hire broad gauge wagons from the Great Western, and it was to be several years before the Severn & Wye owned any rolling stock at all!

In 1869 the Severn & Wye achieved its greatest victory in Parliament when it applied not only for the authorization of the broad gauge line already laid, but also for the construction of the Mineral Loop first mooted in 1868. This was to run from Tufts Junction via Moseley Green and Lightmoor, Crump Meadow and Trafalgar Collieries to an end-on junction with the existing line at Wimberry Junction and to include a branch to connect with the Great Western at Bilson. There was, however, severe opposition from the newly opened Forest of Dean Central Railway and the Great Western, both of whom were worried that the new line would take traffic away from their own. The Severn & Wye countered this by claiming that they were merely providing the collieries with the adequate outlet to the sea, through Lydney harbour, which they required to enable their further development.

The Severn & Wye Act was passed, dated 26th July 1869, and authorized the construction of the Mineral Loop to the broad gauge with the provision that it could be altered to whatever gauge the Great Western should adopt in the future. The Act also stipulated that the tramroad should be maintained alongside the railway in order to join the unconverted sections to Lydney harbour. This, however, appears to have been forgotten in later years as, with the abandonment of the tramroad main line between Speculation and Tufts Junction in 1874, several branches were terminated on interchange wharves such as at Bicslade and Speech House Road. Some of these lines survived for a considerable period, the last being the Bicslade branch which continued in use until 1946.

A further Act of 12th May 1870 was secured to allow the construction of a railway from Serridge Junction to Lydbrook where it was to join the Ross and Monmouth Railway.

Lydney Junction in broad gauge days, looking towards Gloucester. The Severn & Wye line to Lydney Harbour crossed the South Wales main line on the level at this point, having theoretical precedence over the GWR's broad gauge expresses by virtue of the tramroad's prior existence. Although undated, the photograph was obviously taken before the conversion to standard gauge in 1872, whilst the nearer Severn & Wye formation has the appearance of mixed gauge, which existed only between April and May of that year. A wealth of detail of broad gauge practice can be seen including the distinctive goods shed, the early double-sided semaphore signal opposite this, and the pair of shunting horses in the 'down' platform road.

Collection L. E. Copeland

The Severn & Wye properties in Hill Street, Lydney. The nearest building is Severn House which accommodated the S & W offices, and latterly the Joint Committee's Traffic Manager and his staff. Beyond this and set back from the road was the home of two generations of the Keeling family, whilst the cottage next to the level crossing housed the Keelings' coachman. *Rev. D. A. Tipper*

In February 1870 the Company's Secretary called the Directors' attention to the fact that it was likely that some important new works would be built alongside the Dykes branch; this was a private tramroad which ran from its junction with the Severn & Wye tramroad at Tufts Junction to the coal level of Mr. Thomas Dyke. It had been built in 1855 with the Severn & Wye providing the tramplates, the terms of the agreement allowing the Severn & Wye to acquire the branch if they so desired for the cost of its construction, which was stated as being £224. 16s. 2d. for the land and £223. 14s. 11d. for the works. Now the Severn & Wye offered the price of the land but only £100 for the works. This was accepted in March but, due to a clerical error, £111 was in fact paid for the works.

At this time the company also decided that they needed some office accommodation and plans were submitted for a new building at Lydney which, costing some £690, was to become known as Severn House.

In March 1870 another minor landmark in the company's history was reached when Keeling felt compelled to order a goods guards van from the Bristol Wagon Company. His report to the Directors over the matter was almost apologetic, but he stated that a van was necessary to accompany broad gauge trains as it was unsafe to run them without one. The Severn & Wye thus entered the period when it became known as the line with only one item of rolling stock. It was to be a couple more years before any other vehicles joined this solitary brake van on the stock list! At the same Directors' meeting in March a tender was accepted from Messrs. Avonside of Bristol for another new locomotive which, after some delay, was added to stock in December. It was named *Friar Tuck* and like *Robin Hood* was another 0—6—0 side tank convertible. This made a total of five locomotives on the broad gauge as two of the original 0—4—0 tramroad locomotives had been converted, the other two remaining on the tramroad.

Construction of the Mineral Loop was begun in September 1870, the contractor being J. E. Billups of Cardiff. This was about 6½ miles in length and featured some

substantial works including a 503 yard long tunnel at Moseley Green and a viaduct at Pillowell. By November 1869 a broad gauge line had been laid to Mr. H. C. Lückes' Pillowell Colliery along part of the intended route of the loop. However, during the construction of the Mineral Loop, which was intended to be a broad gauge line, the GWR informed the S & W that they intended to convert the South Wales Railway to standard gauge. Keeling therefore decided to lay the Mineral Loop to standard gauge with a third rail from Tufts Junction to Lydney.

Traffic commenced on the new line in April 1872 but only from Crump Meadow Colliery, which was as far as the line had reached. By the middle of May, when the Directors made a trip up the line, it was almost completed to Trafalgar Colliery, and by the middle of June it had reached Wimberry. There it connected with the existing line, which from here to Lydney had been converted to standard gauge as recently as the weekend of 11-12th May. The five broad gauge locomotives were converted to standard gauge and a new standard gauge locomotive *Maid Marian* was delivered from Avonside's in December 1872.

After completing the Mineral Loop Billups moved on to the extension to Lydbrook, which was commenced in June 1872. Again the line involved some substantial works including the 242 yard Mierystock tunnel and a three span wrought iron viaduct across the valley at Lydbrook. The foundation stone of this impressive structure was laid on 9th November 1872, the line being opened for traffic on 26th August 1874 and reported in the *Dean Forest Guardian* as follows:-

RAILWAY EXTENSION

An important local event, although unaccompanied with the least approach to demonstration, took place on Wednesday in the opening of the Lydbrook Railway Extension for traffic. It will be remembered that Lydbrook which is an old Forest village, situated in a deep valley on the northern side of the Ross and Monmouth line, was isolated from any sort of railway accommodation. The principle industries of the valley are Messrs. Thomas Brothers' tin plate works, and some iron forges

Construction work in progress at the site of Lower Lydbrook station prior to the commencement of traffic in 1874. Lydbrook Viaduct has been completed, and towers impressively over the houses in the valley floor, whilst the dumb buffered loco in the platform road probably belongs to the contractor, J. E. Billups of Cardiff.

Collection Rev. D. A. Tipper

A very early view of the S & W main line with broad gauge track alongside the tramroad formation. Although the location has not been positively identified, the lie of the land suggests the site of Travellers Rest crossing. *Collection L. E. Copeland*

belonging to Messrs. Russell. A thriving trade has characterized the place for many years, the first named works having been in existence at least a century. The present branch of railway is one of those promoted by the enterprising Severn & Wye Railway Company and will connect Dean Forest with the Ross and Monmouth line thus affording a most important outlet on the northern side of the Forest. The line at present is purely for mineral traffic but will shortly be opened for passenger service.

Further expansion was authorized by an Act of Parliament of July 1872 which empowered the Severn & Wye to construct a railway to Coleford, from a junction just north of Parkend, and another along the line of Dykes tramroad and up into the Oakwood Valley. Another linking the Oakwood line and the Coleford branch was authorized but not proceeded with.

The Oakwood branch was only extended along the Dykes tramroad as required but the Coleford branch had to be constructed quickly as the Great Western Railway in the same Parliamentary session had promoted their own line to the town, under the guise of the Coleford Railway Company, commencing near Monmouth. Their line was also authorized with the provision that if the Severn & Wye line had not reached the Easter Iron Mine at Milkwall within two years, the Coleford company could extend their own line to that point, a clear violation of Severn & Wye territory.

The contract for the construction of the Coleford branch was let to Messrs. Robinson and Adams of Bristol and the line, which was 3 miles 58 chains in length, mostly clinging to the side of a valley on a gradient of 1 in 30 or 1 in 31, was opened throughout in July 1875.

With the conversion of the main tramroad routes to edge rail, the remainder were generally made redundant,

although the 1869 Act stipulated the continuance of the tramroad connection throughout. The abandonment of the tramroad main line from Speculation Colliery to Tufts Junction was sanctioned by the Commissioners of Woods in January 1874 despite protests from the Wye Colliery Company, the owners of Speculation, about severing the links between their various concerns. The abandonment of the length from Speculation to Lydbrook was also sanctioned apart from the portion connecting Speculation to Mierystock, which was to be retained for the convenience of the Wye Colliery Company.

South of Tufts Junction the tramroad was retained for the use of Richard Thomas and Company, the owners of

A contemporary view to that above, clearly showing the later form of tramroad permanent way, consisting of wrought iron plates held in cast chairs spiked to stone blocks.

Collection L. E. Copeland

several works in the valley and in Lydney, the line not finally being removed until 1883.

An Act passed on the same day as that authorizing the Coleford line, 18th July 1872, was to have a profound effect on the future of the Severn & Wye. It authorized the construction of the Severn Bridge Railway which was to run from a junction with the Great Western at Lydney to Sharpness, crossing the River Severn on a bridge 4,162 feet in length with 21 spans. It was also to join the Severn & Wye by means of a short spur line connecting near Lydney church. A branch from Sharpness to Berkeley Road on the Midland Railway's Birmingham to Bristol main line was to be built by the Midland in order to complete the scheme.

G. W. Keeling was engineer of the Severn Bridge Railway and obviously kept the interests of the Severn & Wye very much in view. In March 1872 the Severn & Wye had been approached to see if they would be willing to work the new line. Their reply was favourable, although they doubted if they could assist financially due to their own heavy expansion programme. By the Act the Severn & Wye, as well as the Great Western, the Midland and the Gloucester & Berkeley Canal Company, were authorized to subscribe to the Severn Bridge concern and all were to do so, apart that is from the Great Western. The Midland took up £50,000 in preference shares and even the Severn & Wye put up £25,000. However, it was the Midland shares which were to prove a great influence on the future of the Severn & Wye.

Construction of the Severn Bridge commenced in 1875 and in the same year passenger services were introduced on the Severn & Wye. These had been authorized by the Act of July 1872, but it was not until a board meeting in May 1873 that it was resolved that 'steps be taken towards the erection of passenger stations at Lydney, Whitecroft, Parkend, Cannop and other places.' In November an estimate for station buildings was received from William Eassie and Company Limited of Gloucester. The buildings were described as 'temporary stations' and, measuring 20′ 0″ x 8′ 6″, were to cost £56. 10s. 0d. each. A week later, on 27th November, Eassie wrote to G. W. Keeling stating that his company could easily erect seven buildings in 6 or 8 weeks from the date of order. The original stations which received these buildings were Lydney Junction, Lydney Town, Whitecroft, Parkend, Speech House Road, and Drybrook Road. One may also have been provided at Upper Lydbrook at this time as the Lydbrook line was then under construction. Similar buildings were also later erected on the Coleford branch at Milkwall and Coleford.

It was originally intended to open the line for passenger traffic in June 1875, but, following the Board of Trade inspection in May, the inspecting officer, Colonel Rich, R.E., directed the Severn & Wye to postpone the opening by one calendar month from 8th June. His report was as follows:

The line is about 12 miles long and is single, with sidings and loops. The gauge is 4 feet 8½ inches and the intervals between the lines of rails, where there are more than one are 6 feet wide. Sufficient land has been enclosed for laying a second line of rails for a distance of about 8 miles. The greater part of the railway was originally constructed as a tramway which was afterwards converted and diverted into a 4 feet 8½ inch gauge railway to convey the coals and other minerals from the Forest of Dean to the port of Lydney. The permanent way consists of a Vignoles pattern rail that weighs about 72 lbs per lineal yard. It is finished and fixed partly in cast iron chairs that weigh 22 lbs each and partly with clips to sleepers laid transversely at an average distance of about 3 feet apart. The chairs and clips are fastened to the sleepers with fang bolts and woodscrews.

The line is ballasted with broken slag, stone and gravel. The steepest gradient is 1 in 40 and the sharpest curve has a radius of 7 chains.

The works consist of three over and six under bridges and 4 viaducts. The Lydbrook Viaduct consists of five stone arches, two openings of 120 feet span and one of 150 feet over which the railway is carried on wrought iron girders of the warren pattern. This viaduct is about 90 feet high. The rest of the bridges and viaducts are of small span and have mostly been constructed for many years. There is a tunnel about 300 yards long. The whole of these works appear to be substantially constructed and of sufficient strength. The two highest piers in the Lydbrook Viaduct show slight settlements in the foundations. I see no reason to apprehend any further settlement in these piers but the cracks should be carefully pointed and watched for some time.

There are five authorized public road level crossings. The stations are Lydbrook Junction, Lower Lydbrook, Upper Lydbrook, Speech House Road, Park End, Whitecroft, Lydney Town and Lydney Junction. They are nearly all situated on steep inclines. There are vertical deviations from 8 in 30 to 9 in 10 and horizontal deviations from 8 in 50 to 8 in 60 outside the Parliamentary limits. No objections have been made to these deviations. The following works require to be executed:-

Lydbrook Junction. The points at the end of the loop line should be set in the reverse direction so as to act as Catch Points. They should be worked from a frame close by, locked with the signals and provided with a bar, or other mechanical contrivance, to prevent their being moved while trains are passing over them. All facing points on the line which have to be worked for passenger trains should be provided with locking bars to prevent the points being moved while trains are passing over them. The home signal should be cleared of intervening trees and hedges or provided with a repeater. The openings into the road near the bridges should be closed.

Lydbrook Viaduct. The small openings in the hand rails next the piers should be closed.

Lower Lydbrook Station. Up home signal to be altered and made clear. A starting signal is required for the siding. A repeater is required for the down distant signal and the view of the up distant signal requires clearing.

The station should be worked with one platform and the loop line should be used as a siding and controlled by catch points. Up goods trains should not be allowed to stop on the passenger line but taken on into the loop line. The points at the south end of the loop line should be set to catch runaway vehicles.

Upper Lydbrook (Cabin A). A repeater is required to up distant signal. Cross over roads should be placed near to the loop points and made to act as a catch for run away vehicles.

Upper Lydbrook (Cabin B). A repeater is required to the down distant signal. The settlement in the abutment of a bridge at 9 M. should be pointed and watched. The rock cutting at the mouth of the tunnel requires clearing of loose and overhanging stones and the rubbish at the top of the rock should be sloped further back.

Mierystock siding up distant signal requires raising and the down distant signal should have a repeater.

Speculation siding. Repeaters to distant signals. **Serridge Junction** — Repeater to up distant signal from Lydbrook. Clear down distant from Lightmoor. No. 8 lever should interlock with No. 2. A starting signal is required for the sidings on the branch and the junction should be arranged so that it shall not be necessary to run the passenger trains backwards on the branch.

Wimblow Junction. A repeater is required for the up distant signal. **Speech House.** Repeater for up distant signal. **Coleford Junction** No. 13 siding signal should interlock with main line signals and points and a starting signal is required for the down line. **Travellers Rest Crossing** The Up home signal should be moved back so as to guard the cross over road and the down home signal should be moved further off so as to guard the siding.

Parkend Siding A repeater is required for the up distant and the down distant signal should be cleared from trees. No. 11 lever should interlock with No. 2. A starting signal is required for the down line. Throw off points to control the tramway crossing. The level crossing gates should be locked but they are too far from the signal cabin for the man stationed there to attend to them.

Whitecroft Station The up distant signal requires to be cleared. **New Mills** The abutment of an overbridge which is supported by struts should be taken down. The up distant signal requires a repeater and the down distant signal should be cleared. The tramway level crossing at 1½ M should be removed. The Middle Forge tramway should be protected with signals if it cannot be removed.

Lydney Town Station Stops are required to prevent the crossing gates opening outwards. One set of facing points should be removed. **Lydney Junction** The tramway level crossing and 3 out of the 5 sets of facing points should be removed. A bridge should be erected to enable the passengers to reach the Booking Office and platforms without walking over the mineral lines. The end of platform near the turntable and the side next the mineral lines should be fenced. The drop into the siding at the back of the Great Western station should also be guarded with stop buffers and a bank.

The Great Western Railway should be protected from the mineral lines which cross it on the level by dead ends the points of which should be interlocked with the signals and the whole should be worked from a raised cabin.

The rails on all the underbridges should be fastened with a proportion of fang bolts, some rails and points require removing and shelter should be provided for passengers on both platforms at the crossing stations. The home signals on this railway cannot generally be seen from the distant signal owing to the curves in the railway and the forest wood through which it runs. Signalmen should be particularly instructed never to commence shunting until the distant signals have been placed at danger for at least 5 minutes. **Clocks** are required at all the stations and signal cabins and guard rails round all curves of less than 10 chains radius.

The Company propose to work the line on the train staff system with the assistance of the block telegraph and with tank engines only as there is only one small turntable at Lydney.

I submit that the Severn and Wye cannot be opened for passenger traffic without danger to the public using the same in consequence of the incomplete state of the works and until satisfactory undertakings as to the proposed mode of workings are sent in.

The Company are not as yet possessed of carriages to convey their passengers but I was informed that they propose to use continuous brakes with all their passenger trains.

I have etc.
(signed) F. M. RICH
Colonel R.E.

G. W. Keeling was quick to respond to certain points raised in Colonel Rich's report, especially with regard to

the crossing over the Great Western at Lydney. It was pointed out to the Board of Trade that in fact it was the Great Western who crossed over the Severn & Wye and that the Severn & Wye trains had precedence over the Great Western.

The re-inspection would have been at the start of July but Keeling wrote to Colonel Rich to say that the line from Serridge to Drybrook Road would not be ready for inspection as no signals or locking gear had yet been fixed on that portion. The line north from Serridge was single line with sidings for Trafalgar Colliery and a terminus station at Drybrook Road Junction which was in fact part of the Mineral Loop. It was intended to run passenger trains from Lydney to Drybrook Road and there run round the train for reversal to Lydbrook, thereby avoiding the need to reverse onto the branch at Serridge.

The Colonel reported again on 13th August but permission to operate passenger trains was still withheld, one of the reasons being that the company still did not possess any carriages. No passenger rolling stock had in fact been ordered from the Gloucester Wagon Company until June — after Colonel Rich's first visit! Two composite and two third class carriages were ordered and at least some of these had been delivered by 18th September when Colonel Rich stated that the Board of Trade 'approve commencement of passenger services. The size of the shed at Lydney Junction should be increased and the starting signals should be placed at the north end of the platform between the two passenger lines. The diagram in the signal cabin requires to be corrected.'

The first passenger train departed at noon on 23rd September from Lydney to Lydbrook and carried the Board of Directors. The *Dean Forest Guardian* reported on the event as follows:

Opening of the Severn & Wye Railway
As announced by posters and otherwise, the first passenger train, upon this important railway, started at noon today (Thursday) from Lydney Junction, drawn by *Robin Hood*. It was most unfortunate that the weather should have been so unfavourable, the rain falling persistently from an early hour until the time for departure. The Directors, however, assembled in force, and headed by Mr. J. Graham Clark, their Chairman, were among the first to avail themselves of this public trip, accompanied by Mr. G. B. Keeling (general manager), Mr. Wintle (solicitor) and Mr. G. W. Keeling, the engineer. The event was signalized by the firing of canon, but apart from this there was no public rejoicing. The stations called at today were Lydney Junction, Lydney Town, Whitecroft, Parkend, Speech House Road, Drybrook Road, Upper Lydbrook, Lower Lydbrook, and Lydbrook Junction.

The train arrived at Lydbrook at 1.20 p.m. and here the Directors 'partook of luncheon'. Despite the rain falling during the journey, the route of the train was lined by Foresters giving it a hearty welcome.

The line to Coleford was opened to passenger traffic on 9th December 1875 following Colonel Rich's inspection. His report was as follows:

The new railway is a single line with sidings at Coleford Junction, at Fetterhill, at Milkwall and at the Coleford Terminal Station. The gauge is 4 feet 8½ inches and the interval between the lines where there are sidings is 6 feet. The length of the new line is 3½ miles, the steepest gradient is 1 in 30 and the sharpest curve has a radius of 8 chains. All curves sharper than

10 chains provided with second rails. The permanent way is similar to that of the Severn and Wye Railway from Lydney to Lydbrook.

The works consist of 2 under and 3 over bridges. One of these latter at Milkwall Junction is a temporary structure of wood. It has to carry a tramway to a colliery until the siding is completed up to the colliery and is sufficient for the purpose. The other works are substantially constructed and of sufficient strength.

The stations on the new line are Milkwall and Coleford.

There is a slight lateral deviation at Coleford and a vertical deviation beyond 5 feet and 2¾-3 miles from Coleford Junction. The landowners have made no objections to these deviations.

Milkwall Station is on a gradient of 1 in 31. The sidings have been arranged and the Company have informed me that no shunting is to be done and no wagons are to be left on the Passenger lines while shunting is being carried on at Fetterhill, the Quarry Sidings or at Milkwall Station.

Catches have been arranged for these sidings but not on the passenger lines as the Company do not like to make loops and place facing points on the falling inclines of 1 in 31 of which the greater part of the new railway consists.

The following works are required.

The path to Coleford Station should be fenced from the Goods Shed to the platform and one directing post should be placed at the entrance yard gate and a second near the goods shed and the two sidings at the north east side of the goods shed should be banked up at the end.

Diagrams and clocks are required in the station signal cabins and the levers that work the points and signals should be numbered. A urinal is required at Milkwall Station. An old quickset hedge at the summit of the railway between Milkwall and Coleford stations requires to be laid and trimmed and a post and rail or 3 wires fixed to posts should be run along it as it is at present in a weak state and cattle might break through it.

Mr. Keeling the Engineer of the Railway has promised to have these small things executed at once. I enclose an undertaking as to the proposed mode of working which is satisfactory and I submit that the Board of Trade may sanction the opening of the Coleford Branch of the Severn and Wye Railway for passenger traffic. The Railway owing to the sharp curves and continuous heavy gradient should be worked with great care.

F. H. RICH (COLONEL R.E.)

The first passenger train to Coleford received a rapturous welcome, the town having waited over 20 years since the first proposal. It arrived at Coleford at 1 p.m. and a luncheon followed at the Town Hall with festivities continuing into the night.

At first the Severn & Wye passenger services were reasonably intensive. Five trains a day ran in each direction on the Lydney to Lydbrook section, although two of these only ran between Lydney and Parkend and one between Drybrook Road and Lydbrook. On the Coleford branch, the passenger service in January 1876 consisted of two trains a day between Lydney and Coleford together with one 'down' and two 'up' connections with main line trains at Coleford Junction. However, by December 1875 the second class had been abolished and the Lydney-Lydbrook service was cut to three trains a day, the last of which ran only as far as Drybrook Road. Even this was cut in July 1879 to one train a day plus one to Upper Lydbrook only. At the same time the service on the Coleford branch was trimmed to one through train each way, together with the main line connections.

Drybrook Road served as the local station for Cinderford, which, besides Lydney and Coleford, was the only other town of any size in the Forest. However, the station was still 1½ miles from the town and inevitably the subject of local complaints. The Severn & Wye consequently constructed a 'drop Platform' at 9 miles 65 chains alongside the branch to Bilson, almost half a mile further on, with the ultimate intention of building a permanent station at Bilson. The platform was a temporary measure as any extension of passenger services beyond this point would entail running over the Trafalgar Colliery Company's locomotive tramway. This crossed the Severn & Wye on the level and Keeling realized that they would not readily be able to make the necessary arrangements to satisfy the Board of Trade.

On 19th July 1876 Keeling wrote to the Board of Trade advising them of the new platform and asking for permission to bring it into use. Passengers were to be carried to and from the platform in the train but booked at Drybrook Road. The inspecting officer reported that the line was on a 1 in 55.8 incline and stipulated that the single carriage intended to be used by the company must be braked or accompanied by a brake van. He was evidently not keen on this arrangement and sanctioned it for one year only while a new station was being built on a level part of the branch and 'this exceptional state of working done away with'. The halt, known as Bilson Platform, was opened to traffic in September 1876.

Plans for the new arrangements were submitted to the Board of Trade in November that year but as the new station was not completed until 1878 an extension of time was granted for the continuing use of the drop platform. The new Cinderford station, on the northern spur of the triangular junction with the Great Western at Bilson, was sanctioned for use and replaced Bilson Platform on 29th August 1878.

In 1878 the Severn & Wye reached a most crucial turning point after which the company's fortunes, although never great, were to suffer. The building of the Severn Bridge was progressing well but more money was required to complete the venture. A call was made upon the preference shares but the Midland Railway refused to take up its options unless it was given running powers over the entire Severn & Wye system. They had attempted to gain this facility in 1873 but the offer of reciprocal running powers for the Severn & Wye as far as Bristol was rejected. The Severn & Wye Board were worried about their relationship with the Great Western which surrounded them on three sides and to whom they could always sell out in the future.

At a meeting of the Severn & Wye and the Severn Bridge companies it was decided that, in order to save the bridge, the two companies should be amalgamated and that the Midland Railway should be granted the running powers it requested. In return the Severn & Wye was granted running powers to Stroud and Nailsworth. However, these powers had little effect as, on the opening of the Severn Bridge line in October 1879, Severn & Wye trains merely ran through to Berkeley Road and later some Midland passenger services ran as far as Coleford.

The Severn & Wye and the Severn Bridge companies were amalgamated by an Act of Parliament of 21st July

An early postcard view of the Severn Bridge with the station of that name visible on the approach embankment. When opened in 1879 the bridge enabled Forest of Dean and South Wales coal to be shipped from the deep water port at Sharpness. An attempt was also made to exploit the coal trade to the South Coast and West Country, but this was greatly reduced by the opening of the GWR's Severn Tunnel route.

Collection N. Parkhouse

1879 to form the Severn & Wye and Severn Bridge Railway Company, but it was not until 1885 that they were fully unified. Until this time the accounts of the two halves were kept quite separate and there were still two Boards of Directors forming the 'Wye section' and the 'Bridge section'.

Upon the commencement of passenger services across the bridge, the old Severn & Wye terminus was replaced by a station at Lydney Junction situated on the new curve connecting the two lines. The first timetable for the amalgamated companies included seven trains in each direction to and from Berkeley Road. Of the 'down' trains from Berkeley Road two went through to Lydbrook Junction, four only as far as Lydney Junction and one to Cinderford with connecting services to Coleford. The 'up' trains to Berkeley Road consisted of one from Coleford, three from Lydney Junction, two from Lydbrook Junction and one from Cinderford, together with further connections from Coleford branch trains.

By 1879, therefore, the Severn & Wye in the preceding decade had converted the vast majority of its tramroad system to edge rail, built new lines and introduced passenger services. Its amalgamation with the Severn Bridge Railway had provided an important route out of the confines of the Forest but in securing this the company had lost some of its independence to the Midland.

The reconstruction of the system had cost the company a great deal of money, much of which had been raised by the Directors in the form of bank loans with personal liability. Throughout the 1870s, however, trade was depressed within the Forest, especially in the iron and iron-ore trade, due to foreign competition. Several miners' strikes also hit the company's revenue. To enable the repayment of loans and interest, an extension of capital of £30,000 was sanctioned in 1876, but of the 3,000 £10 shares only 191 were taken up. This share issue was superseded in 1877 when a further Act increased the capital by £60,000.

In 1877 proposals to reduce expenditure were put before the Board. These involved the dismissal of several employees and the loan to James Caldwell, a carter, of an 'old horse' to enable him to perform a carrier's service around Lydney on the company's behalf. The estimated saving to the company of these proposals was around £885 per annum. In an attempt to increase passenger traffic by attracting tourists, the Severn & Wye had some posters 'lithographed in colours' for distribution around the country. The order was placed in April 1880 and by July offers to exhibit them were arriving from other railway companies. The Great Northern agreed to take six, the Metropolitan and District four, the London & South Western Railway allowed them to be placed at as many stations as the Severn & Wye wished, the London, Chatham & Dover took twenty, the Midland were going to place them at all principal stations, but the neighbouring Great Western, by which most tourists would probably reach the Severn & Wye, only agreed to take twenty. The following year the Directors resolved to publish a tourist handbook showing the delights of the Forest as, having attracted some tourists, they wished to enable them to know what they were looking at! It was published by John Bellows of Gloucester but the Severn & Wye subsidized it at the rate of 2d per copy, reducing to 1d over 2,000 copies.

Over the years various excursion trains were run, some of them even prior to the commencement of passenger services. An account of one of these appeared in the *Gloucester Citizen* in January 1948 when a Mr. Samuel Thomas reminisced:

> There were no coaches in those days; the women were accommodated in six cattle trucks, and the menfolk and boys occupied six open wagons. Before the journey, the men had to prepare the train themselves and arrange seating accommodation, and so keen were the local staff that lots were drawn to decide who should do duty on the engine. On that occasion, Lydney Brass Band were engaged to accompany the party and to play rousing music as the train steamed through the woods and villages, watched by crowds who lined the route. By the time the trippers reached home at night, it is said that the band had completely exhausted their repertoire.

In latter years the company had to purchase extra second-hand coaching stock in order to be able to supply the demands of the excursion traffic.

In September 1882 the General Manager reported that, in consequence of the scarcity of labour, a colliers' train was to be introduced from Lydney, Whitecroft and Parkend to Drybrook Road. This left Lydney at 6 a.m., the miners returning by the public service at 3.50 p.m., and as this was apparently accomplished without running any extra trains, presumably passenger vehicles were attached to an existing goods service. Brass cheques were issued to the owners of the collieries who in turn distributed them to the men in return for the fare which was then passed on to the Severn & Wye.

In March 1883, however, a colliers strike began which lasted about six weeks and had a serious effect on the Severn & Wye. While the strike was on the company made every effort to reduce expenditure by putting all the men in the locomotive and traffic departments on short time working. All repairs were stopped as was all relaying on the main line, which was a continuous process as, since 1877, about two miles of the original iron rails were replaced by steel ones every year and the programme was not completed until 1890. This strike and previous ones drastically reduced the company's revenue and prevented them from discharging dues on the debentures. A High Court judgement was gained against the company by Edmund Viner Ellis of Gloucester and the Severn & Wye was forced into liquidation.

The General Manager and the Secretary were appointed joint receivers and the Directors became managers. All receipts from the company had to be declared to the Court which then advised distribution.

In February 1884 the Court was asked to create a reserve fund for the renewal of locomotives and rolling stock which it was stated were rapidly becoming old. In March an application was made to the Court that, before any division of funds was made, a sum not exceeding

A Severn & Wye poster portraying the attractions of the Forest of Dean together with a map of the railway system. A similar one may be seen outside the booking office at Lydney Town station in the photograph on page 21. The poster was reprinted in 1892 following requests from other railway companies who wished to display it.

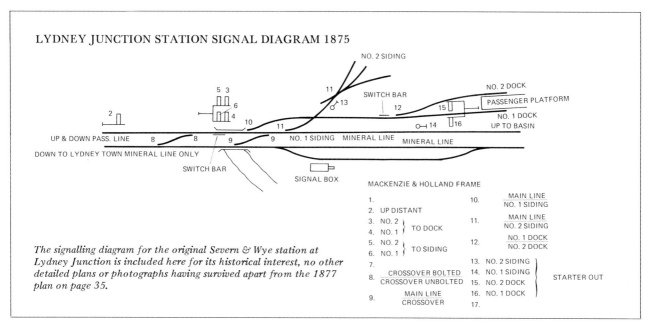

LYDNEY JUNCTION STATION SIGNAL DIAGRAM 1875

The signalling diagram for the original Severn & Wye station at Lydney Junction is included here for its historical interest, no other detailed plans or photographs having survived apart from the 1877 plan on page 35.

£2,500 should be spent to restore the line 'to a condition indispensable for the security of its traffic' as, because of a depression in trade, this was a favourable time to buy steel rails at very low rates.

In May 1884 the Severn Bridge Directors resolved that a reorganization and amalgamation of the stocks and shares of the undertaking should be carried out so that the Wye and Bridge sections could be fused into one, but objections were raised by the Severn & Wye Directors. In January 1885, owing to the inability of the two sets of Directors to reach an agreement concerning the amalgamation, a circular was sent to shareholders setting out the two proposals and on 24th April an Extraordinary General Meeting was held at the Park Hotel, Bristol. The period of receivership was brought to an end when a scheme of arrangement was enrolled on 21st July 1885 under which the two sections were completely united and all debentures were converted into four per cent stock.

In an attempt to save further monies, the company had approached the Office of Woods in May 1885 with the view of obtaining a reduction in the rent paid for land leased from the Crown. This was agreed and the total rent was reduced for a period of 3 years from £523 to £348 per annum. A note attached to an Office of Woods memorandum reveals that the Crown believed that the difficulties the Severn & Wye were in were caused by the amalgamation with the Severn Bridge Railway 'which has turned out so disastrously.' The reduced rent actually continued until 1894 following two further appeals to the Crown at 3 year intervals.

Throughout 1886 and 1887 the industries of the Forest continued through a period of depression. Concerned to encourage trade, particularly via the Severn Bridge route, the Severn & Wye erected new coal tips at Sharpness Docks. A deep water tip was provided for Welsh coal, utilizing the existing Forest coal tip, which was itself replaced by a new structure. The contractor was J. E. Billups, who had constructed the Mineral Loop and Lyd-

brook extension, and the tips were completed by July 1886.

At the same time, the Severn & Wye's shipping agent, J. V. Thomas, was sent to Ireland to 'canvass merchants and ship owners to send their vessels to Sharpness for Forest coal'.

A nightly coal train taking Welsh coal from Aberdare to Southampton, and later Portsmouth, had been running since 1883, although traffic was irregular and the train often failed to run. This was largely due to the Great Western's reluctance to grant through rates to stations south of Gloucester via the Severn Bridge, which discouraged traders from using the route.

By June 1885 the Severn & Wye had become anxious to obtain through rates before the Severn Tunnel opened, and had decided to apply to the Railway Commissioners for the necessary orders. Despite fierce Great Western opposition, the Railway Commissioners decided in favour of the Severn & Wye, recommending the application of through rates for Forest coal and Welsh coal from the 1st and 18th April 1886 respectively.

This was not to be the end of the story, however, as the Great Western were clearly determined to put as many obstacles as possible in the way of the Severn Bridge route, at first refusing to instruct their station masters until the written order was received. In addition the Great Western insisted that all receipts for traffic exchanged between the two companies should be divided by the Railway Clearing House, and would not agree to the Severn & Wye's accountant performing this task in order to save the Clearing House expense.

Finally the Great Western refused the Severn & Wye's request for through rates to stations situated between those actually specified by the Commissioners. By August 1886 the Great Western had, rather grudgingly, offered through rates to 30 of the 56 stations applied for, but at higher rates than the Severn & Wye proposed and only until the Severn Tunnel opened, when they were to cease.

A postcard view showing a busy scene in the upper basin of Lydney Docks, looking back towards the Junction station. Coal tips 3, 4 and 5 are visible on the left whilst a line of Forest colliery wagons can be seen on the Upper Docks branch to the right. Lydney Docks provided a major outlet for Forest coal to a number of ports in the West Country. *Collection N. Parkhouse*

However, when the Severn & Wye filed a further application with the Railway Commissioners, the Great Western came to terms immediately, presumably confident that the opening of the tunnel would effectively finish the Severn Bridge as a through route. Through rates were therefore agreed for all the stations in question, except for a small number which the Severn & Wye had offered to exclude, and these came into force on 3rd August 1886.

Unfortunately the Severn & Wye's victory was both hollow and short-lived as, amidst great publicity, the Severn Tunnel opened for traffic on 1st September 1886, offering a fast direct route to the South-West for the lucrative South Wales coal traffic.

The Great Western, not surprisingly, were quick to capitalize on their new asset. The Southampton coal train was cancelled from 31st August 1886, and new Forest coal rates via the tunnel were issued which were between 1d and 10d per ton below the rates via the Severn Bridge.

To give an extra twist to the knife, the Great Western also reduced rates from Bilson, on their Forest of Dean branch, to Great Western stations not affected by the Severn Bridge, thereby hitting at Severn & Wye traffic to the Midlands.

Although the Severn & Wye and Midland agreed to split the difference in allowances in order to make the bridge and tunnel rates the same, it was necessary for the Severn & Wye to place canvassers in the West of England and at the Forest collieries in order to gain trade and check the routing of traffic.

A fresh application, with Midland assistance, was made to the Railway Commissioners to resolve the matter, whilst the Great Western countered this by applying to rescind all through rates. On the 30th December 1886 the Commissioners passed judgement as follows:

1. South Wales coal rates were rescinded.

2. The Great Western application to rescind Forest rates was refused with costs.

3. The Severn & Wye's application to apply tunnel rates to the bridge route was granted without costs.

Having resisted throughout the hearing, the Great Western now agreed to the Severn & Wye's proposal to raise the tunnel rates to those applying via the bridge route, and this came into force in February 1887.

Although the Severn and Wye had met with considerable success in proceeding before the Railway Commissioners, it had cost the company some £1200, and failed to prevent further wrangles with the Great Western over through rates, which continued throughout 1887.

During this time the Great Western's determination in cutting rates, combined with the natural advantages of the Severn Tunnel route, also led to a decline in the Severn & Wye's passenger traffic to Bristol and shipping traffic from Lydney Docks.

In 1888 the coal trade was considerably down, thereby hitting the Severn & Wye receipts once more. Difficulties were obviously being encountered in meeting certain demands as, at a Board meeting in July, there was some discussion as to what would happen if traffic was seized in lieu of income tax. Whether it was a prophetic discussion or if it was known that a tax demand could not be met is unknown, but a couple of weeks later a loaded wagon was seized at Lydney Junction by Mr. Alfred Pope the local tax inspector!

Not only were the financial affairs of the Severn & Wye in a run down state but also the locomotive stock. By this time the company owned thirteen locomotives, all of which were 0–6–0 tanks with the exception of one 0–4–0. Additions to stock had been made over the years to cope with the extensions to the system and increases in traffic. The only disposals had been the original five tramroad locomotives. In November 1891 a report by Mr. Owen, Locomotive Superintendent of the Brecon and Merthyr Railway, was considered at a special meeting of the Severn & Wye finance committee. As a result of the report the locomotive foreman, J. Conquest, was superannuated and great blame for the state of the locomotives was attached to R. Turner, the leading boilersmith, as it appeared that the locomotive fireboxes had been badly neglected. The General Manager was instructed to report to the Board every month on the condition of the locomotives and he was also authorized to seek a new locomotive foreman.

In 1892 John Anderson of Glasgow, late locomotive superintendent of the Quebrade Railway in South America, was appointed the new locomotive foreman, and he, together with his assistant, J. Crelling, soon improved the locomotive situation.

The trade depression continued into the 1890s and a series of industrial disputes in the coal industry began in 1892. In February 1893 the Directors announced that the continuing depression in the Forest of Dean coal trade was seriously affecting the company's receipts and preventing the payment of dividends on preference stocks. Furthermore by July some of the Forest collieries had stopped production as the proprietors found it impossible to make a profit.

The company's financial position was considered at a Board meeting on 18th July, when it was stated that coal from competing districts had displaced Forest coal in the markets due to the fact that colliers in other areas had taken a drop in wages and the price of coal had consequently been greatly reduced. In the Forest wages had remained the same and as a result the principal Forest collieries had, during the past half year, not been working more than two or three days a week with inevitable effects on the Severn & Wye. The Directors pointed out that these were circumstances entirely beyond the control of the company and that, in the interests of all concerned, it would be best to seek the protection of the Court. It was consequently resolved that once again steps should be taken to secure the appointment of a receiver. The Secretary was instructed not to pay the half-year's interest due in August and to call upon the guaranteeing companies to provide the interest on £75,000 of guaranteed 4 per cent debenture stock.

It was arranged that E. Viner Ellis should once again obtain a judgement against the company. Viner Ellis was Vice-Chairman of the Sharpness Docks Company, one of the guaranteeing companies, and he agreed to institute proceedings, it being arranged that he should use a different firm of solicitors to the Severn & Wye. In fact he used the same firm as in 1883. The necessary order was

Friar Tuck receiving attention to its motion at Berkeley Road station prior to working back onto the Severn & Wye system via the Midland branch to Sharpness. Built in 1870 by Avonside's of Bristol, the loco was transferred to the MR in 1895, ending its days at Derby. The coach is one of the S & W's three brake thirds, built by the Gloucester Wagon Company in 1875-6.   *L & GRP, courtesy David & Charles*

obtained in the High Court on 5th August, the General Manager and Secretary again being appointed receivers and the Directors, managers.

It would appear that the locomotives were again being neglected as, in January 1893, Anderson sent a report to the Board stating that it was necessary to purchase another engine to enable him to send engines to the shed for repairs. In February the General Manager also pointed out the urgent need to purchase a new engine to enable the repairs of 'the old engines' to be kept up. In the midst of these problems the shed staff had, by August 1893, been put on short time as an economy measure, but they were soon reinstated after protests from Anderson who pointed out that this made matters even worse.

The Forest house coal collieries re-opened on 18th September to a staggering rise in demand. A prolonged strike in Derbyshire brought about a complete reversal of prosperity and demand for Forest coal became very high, as apparently did its prices. In fact their output was so great that the Severn & Wye had difficulty in coping with the traffic and it became necessary to pay the Midland to work some of it from Lydney Junction to Sharpness. In November it was reported that the traffic was more than the company's engines and men could cope with and an engine had to be hired from the Midland. In addition traders were threatening legal proceedings because of delays in the delivery of their wagons.

At a Board meeting in October 1893 George White, a major stockholder, revealed that in 1890 he had approached the Midland Railway to see if they would be interested in purchasing the Severn & Wye. After inspecting the line the Midland declined, claiming that about £20,000 would be required to bring it up to standard. White then stated that he had recently approached the Great Western, only to find that they already knew of his overtures to the Midland. The Great Western subsequently contacted the Midland who expressed their willingness to join the Great Western in joint purchase of the undertaking.

Their offer evidently impressed White, who claimed that the terms were the highest available and urged the Directors to come to an immediate and favourable decision, as it was necessary that the Parliamentary notices should appear by 11th November. After White had left the meeting there was considerable discussion during which it was suggested that the LNWR and the LSWR should be approached. However, this was rejected in case it frightened off the Great Western and the Midland!

In the meantime, continuing heavy traffic made it necessary to hire six wagons in December to supply extra loco coal and the hired Midland engine was retained until at least February. In the same month the proposals for the purchase were approved at a special Board meeting. The terms of the sale agreement were:-

1. The purchase money to be £477,300 to be paid to the liquidators on 2nd July 1894.

2. The Severn & Wye to realize their assets and discharge their liabilities.

3. The expenses of liquidating the company and distributing the purchase money to be borne by the Severn & Wye.

4. The present receivers to be the liquidators.

It seems ironical that the sale should come about when the railway was so hard pressed to cope with the traffic boom. It was also sad that after 47 years dedicated to the Severn & Wye, George Baker Keeling died on 28th February 1894, the day after the meeting, in the knowledge that the company which he had steered so well through good and bad times was about to pass into the hands of the larger monopolies. As has been seen, he had joined the

GEORGE WILLIAM KEELING

Severn & Wye Railway & Canal Company in 1847 as clerk, later he became Secretary, and in 1871 Secretary and General Manager. He resigned from this post at the time of the amalgamation with the Severn Bridge Railway, and was re-elected to the Board and at the time of his death was Managing Director.

G. B. Keeling was replaced as General Manager by his son George William Keeling, who until this time had been Engineer. It was G. W. Keeling who had introduced locomotives onto the tramroad, overseen the conversion of the line to edge rail, expanded the system, built the Severn Bridge and introduced passenger services. Under the new management he resumed responsibility for the locomotive department.

The Parliamentary Bill necessary for the sale was only passed after considerable opposition from various quarters which included Richard Thomas & Company, the Gloucester & Berkeley Navigation, the Corporations of Gloucester and Newport, the Sharpness New Docks Company, Sir James Campbell and Charles Bathurst. The Bill received the Royal Assent and the Severn & Wye & Severn Bridge Railway was jointly vested in the Great Western and Midland Railways from 1st July 1894.

CHAPTER THREE

THE JOINT COMMITTEE
1894-1923

UNDER the new joint ownership a committee of three directors from each company administered not only the newly acquired Severn & Wye but also the Clifton Extension Railway, Halesowen Railway and the joint stations at Bristol, Churchdown, Worcester and Great Malvern. On the ground a traffic manager for the Severn & Wye, John J. Petrie, was appointed by the Midland in 1895.

The poor condition of the S & W locos and rolling stock has already been mentioned but at first it was decided to retain them. The responsibility for their maintenance fell to the MR, who also supplied loco coal and other loco stores, whilst the GWR maintained the permanent way, signals and telegraph, and other works. Cash receipts, accounts and payments of wages were divided into two sections, Berkeley Road to Lydney inclusive being controlled by the Midland, and the remainder by the GWR. The original arrangements, however, were short-lived.

In 1895 the GWR recommended that the engines and stock and even the locomotive department staff be abolished and replacements hired from the parent companies, but the Midland wanted to replace them only as it became necessary. The Great Western persisted and in July suggested they should provide locos for a period of 3 years at the following rates:

Passenger trains	6½d per train mile
Goods trains	8d per train mile
Shunting	4/- per hour

Any loco provided by the MR was subject to the same rates. This was agreed and put into effect for 10 years from 1st October 1895, each company providing new rolling stock. It was also agreed that MR coaching stock was to be almost solely employed on the Berkeley branch, GW coaches not being used unless requested by the MR. The existing stock of engines, passenger carriages, goods wagons and even machinery from Lydney works, was subsequently valued and divided equally between the two companies. Although some of the GWR's locos lingered for a few years on the Severn & Wye system, these eventually suffered the same fate as their Midland counterparts,

A Berkeley Road bound passenger train at Lydney Town c.1894-5. The loco is *Robin Hood*, built by Fletcher Jennings in 1868 and shown here as later modified with cab and rear weatherboard, the latter doing little to improve its appearance. The original Eassie/Gloucester Wagon Co. buildings, complete with Severn & Wye 'ephemera', can clearly be seen.   *Collection Rev. D. A. Tipper*

19

GWR '2021' class 0–6–0ST No. 2039 pauses outside the newly constructed signal box at Tufts Junction before proceeding up the Oakwood branch with empties for Princess Royal Colliery. This box was provided in 1896 whilst No. 2039 was built in February 1898 and almost certainly supplied new to Lydney shed, the photograph probably being taken very soon after this.

Collection Mrs. Knight

being dispersed to various parts of the parent companies' system. The coaching stock appears to have been scrapped almost immediately, whilst the fate of the goods stock is not recorded.

Soon after its inception the Joint Committee received a communication from the Board of Trade concerning the hours worked by signalmen, station masters and others who performed signalling duties. In response Keeling was instructed to arrange to reduce their shifts to within 12 hours a day and confer with the two companies over the extra staff necessary to achieve this. The superintendents of each company also visited the line to examine the traffic department staff and recommend those suitable for permanent employment, and the MR, who also provided ropes, traffic stores and general stationery, supplied uniforms lettered 'Mid & GW'. (Curiously from 1912 the Great Western supplied mackintoshes to all relevant grades of S & W staff.)

The Act authorizing the sale of the Severn & Wye obliged its new owners to build an extension to Cinderford, taking the line right into the town, within four years. Local people had pressed for this for some years and to this end Messrs. Lambert and Turner met a deputation at Cinderford on 14th June 1895 when the town's recreation ground was mutually agreed as the site for the new terminus. The necessary powers were sought in the ensuing session of Parliament (the Bill including the transfer of the Sharpness branch to the Joint Committee) and the £15,000 contract for the line's construction was placed with Mr. Braddock of Manchester in February 1898.

In the meantime, in April 1896, Petrie pointed out the need to double the line between Tufts Junction and Parkend to cope with the traffic. The former Severn & Wye Co. had put this in hand as long ago as 1891, when it is recorded that work had commenced and 'would gradually be completed'. By August 1893 it was reported that the doubling work near Whitecroft had been suspended, and doubtless the company's financial struggles prevented them from completing it. Now the committee's decision was prompted by the need to spend some £348 on signalling. However, as the ground was already levelled, little work was involved, the estimated cost being:

Doubling P.W.	£1,565
Locking and Signals	680
Telegraphs	53
	£2,298

A fascinating view of the station staff at Lydney Town in a photograph contemporary with that on page 19. The staff are wearing uniforms supplied by the Midland Railway which are basically standard MR with different insignia. The three porters to the left have no visible insignia, whilst the ticket collector to their right appears to have the 'joint' insignia on his cap. Station master W. A. Taylor, third from right, has no cap insignia but 'joint' insignia on his coat lapels, and the porter to the extreme right has standard MR headgear. The bowler-hatted gentleman fourth from right may possibly be the Severn & Wye's cartage agent, but the identity and function of the two individuals (and dog!) seated on the platform trolley is open to conjecture. The station buildings are shown in greater detail here, whilst in the background may be glimpsed Lydney Town crossing in its original form prior to the addition of a footbridge and signal box in 1897.

Collection M. Rees

The new station at Cinderford seen in around 1905 from the Station Hotel. Opened in 1900 in order to extend Severn & Wye passenger services into the town, the station was connected to the GWR's Forest of Dean branch by 1907 and it was this latter service from Newnham which finally outlasted the S & W by almost 30 years. The incoming train is hauled by one of the ubiquitous '2021' class saddle tanks, and waiting for it is a large funeral party complete with horse-drawn hearse. Although the station is essentially Great Western in character, being built to a standard GWR design, Midland influence is nevertheless apparent by virtue of the wagons in the foreground and the milk van in the goods shed entrance. *Collection A. K. Pope*

A Lydney Town train arriving at Sharpness station which was originally built as part of the Midland branch from Berkeley Road. The coaches are those supplied by the Midland, whilst the '2021' class saddle tank is unusual in that it has an extended 'drumhead' smokebox.

Lens of Sutton

The work was approved, but the substitution of new rails instead of secondhand ones, extra ballast and retaining walls to avoid interference with the bridleway alongside, caused the figures to be exceeded by £532 10s. 0d.

The doubling was completed in August 1898 and inspected by the Board of Trade on 20th November. It was, however, subject to further improvements as detailed on page 115, and finally approved on 19th December 1899.

The Cinderford extension was completed and opened for public traffic on 2nd July 1900 and inspected on 5th July 1900. The new station was not only a vast improvement, but a far more fitting terminus for the 'main line' than its rather primitive predecessor which closed to passengers on the same day.

The working of the S & W was under constant review by the parent companies and by 1897 it was pointed out that the cumulative mileage of the carriages was somewhat unbalanced, the GW stock earning some £993 against some £626 of the MR. Petrie was instructed to regulate his requisitions for carriages to equalize earnings but it was not until 1899 that the MR mileage finally caught up, but the correcting bias was maintained until the MR mileage exceeded the GW, and Petrie's successor, J. A. Carter, was again instructed to remedy this. Carter, incidentally, became traffic manager in 1898 and remained so until the end of 1919, when both he and the S & W's accountant, K. W. Doughty, retired. Management of the line from 1st January 1920 was thereafter undertaken by the parent companies as per the division of maintenance.

As a result of this the majority of the former Severn & Wye offices at Lydney Town became surplus to requirements, and arrangements were made for the MR to let the vacant space.

Both MR and GW coaches ran together in various combinations, but complaints from the public in 1902 about the absence of carriage heating drew the committee's attention to the incompatibility of the heating equipment. The GW steam heating was not interchangeable with MR appliances so the MR agreed to supply alternative coaches.

It has to be said that the MR stock was far superior to the GW and much preferred by the passengers for comfort. Most of the coaches were usually kept under cover and generally cleaned and well cared for. Vandalism was not tolerated and when on 3rd December 1903 a local man cut off and stole a leather window strap from one of the Midland vehicles, he was sentenced to two months imprisonment with hard labour — a far cry from today.

After the first ten years of the committee, running arrangements were again reviewed and this time it was decided to divide the maintenance of the permanent way, telegraphs, signalling, etc. equally between the two companies. Therefore, as from 21st January 1906, the GW took responsibility for the maintenance of the line north from a point 6 chains south of Coleford Junction, including the Mineral Loop, whilst the MR looked after the remainder. The staff in these departments were transferred to the respective companies and the signalling of the junctions with the GW was maintained by that company at the committee's expense. The MR continued to supply clothing at cost plus 7½%, as on other GW and MR joint lines, and the GW continued to supply tickets. An interesting point from these arrangements is that staff on the new MR and GW sections had to adopt their respective company's book of rules and regulations. The agreement whereby the GW supplied motive power for ten years expired on 30th September 1905 and, when this was renewed, mileage rates were dropped in favour of hourly charges of 5/6d to the committee.

With the passing of the 1904 Dean Forest Mines Act and the ensuing development of the deeper coal measures, coal traffic on the Severn & Wye increased following the opening of Cannop and Arthur & Edward Collieries and the further development of Princess Royal. In this connection improvements had to be made to the facilities at Speech House Road and Serridge Junction.

Following a more general policy of opening a number of additional stopping places or halts, the Great Western decided in 1907 to introduce a motor passenger service over their mineral branch between Newnham and Drybrook. They also wished to build a new connecting loop with the S & W and run into Cinderford station. The committee agreed on the understanding that the entire cost of construction, maintenance, renewal and working of the new junction was borne by the GW who also agreed

that for use of the joint line between the new junction and Cinderford station, the joint committee was to be credited 'with a one mile proportion of gross receipts from traffic carried in GW trains . . . GW to contribute a share of interest at the rate of 4% per annum on the total cost of the station and of maintenance and working expenses in the ratio to which the number of their trains bear to the total number of trains using the station — 2 GW motor units being reckoned for this purpose as equivalent to one train of the Joint Committee.'

The Great Western did not delay, advising the Board of Trade of their intention on 31st December that year and completing the work the following March. The new curve, 31 chains long and 12 chains in radius, rising 1 in 51 from Bilson Junction to the new 'Cinderford Junction' on the S & W, was inspected by the Board of Trade on 6th April 1908 and brought into use on the same day.

The Severn and Wye had thus reached full development although, particularly in comparison to most other lines, it was continually changing. Private sidings came and went with the rise and fall of local industries and traffic fluctuated according to their success. However, of the many changes perhaps the most notable was the demise of the Great Western branch to Coleford, leaving only the Severn & Wye route. The GW branch was closed and lifted during the First World War and never reinstated.

A southbound Severn & Wye passenger train at Speech House Road station in Joint Committee Days.
Lens of Sutton

CHAPTER FOUR

AFTER THE GROUPING
1923-47

AS far as the Severn and Wye was concerned, the 1923 Grouping had little if any effect. The Midland Railway was vested into the newly formed London Midland & Scottish Railway and the Joint Committee simply continued between the GW and LMS and was in fact formed of the same representatives as from the MR and GWR. However, the years ahead were lean times and with increasing road competition, the need for economy was paramount.

In a sustained effort to improve operating efficiency, a careful watch was kept on the deployment of motive power. Fluctuations in mineral traffic were inevitable with the varying output from each of the collieries and two services, the 6.45 p.m. Lydney to Lightmoor and back, and the 10.00 p.m. Lydney to Sharpness and back, were stopped whenever traffic was light, but the irregular running of these trains resulted in a certain amount of waste in engine power. The Great Western were concerned about this and the Joint Committee agreed to discontinue the services concerned from 2nd September 1925, the Lydney docks shunting engine also being booked for 2½ hours less each day from the same date.

At a committee meeting on 1st February the following year, it was pointed out that despite the withdrawal of the two trains there had been no corresponding decrease in engine power. It was said that although some older collieries had reduced their output, the same number of clearances were still required and furthermore the depression in coal trade had indirectly increased shunting requirements at Lydney and Sharpness docks because of the larger quantities of shipment coal stabled there. It was therefore decided that everything had been done to curtail engine power which had already been reduced from 29,720 hours for the latter half of 1923 (28 weeks) to 26,582 hours for the corresponding period in 1925.

The Severn and Wye had run at a loss in 1922 and, although the annual working expenses had been reduced from £121,249 in 1922 to £108,711 in 1927, the line made another loss in 1927. Clearly greater economy measures were called for and it was decided that the withdrawal of passenger services would have the most effect, despite additional station accommodation at Coleford being approved on 9th October 1924. Although coal traffic had increased, passenger receipts had practically halved since 1922 because of intensive road competition. As the Severn Bridge was the only link with the other side of the estuary, it was decided to maintain the service between Berkeley Road and Lydney but provide motor buses to replace the service north of Lydney Town.

The signal box at Cinderford was taken out of use on 17th May 1927 and the section from Cinderford Junction to Cinderford worked by wooden train staff in lieu of the electric train token system. The signal box at Drybrook Road was converted to a ground frame on the same date.

Staff economies recommended in March 1928 were put into immediate effect (only six men made redundant) but it was calculated that the withdrawal of passenger services would enable a reduction in engine power, enginemen and shed staff, trainmen's hours, compression of freight service, regrading of signalmen (reduced to porter/signalmen) and reduced engineering and signal department charges.

More detailed proposals were discussed at a meeting on 9th March the following year when it was proposed that the withdrawal of passenger services would produce the following savings:-

10 GWR 4-wheeled coaches and 8 LMS 8-wheeled coaches reduced to 4 vehicles from each company.

14 engines reduced to 11.

24 enginemen reduced to 19.

29 guards reduced to 25.

Engine hours reduced from 983 hours per week to 807.

Numerous other staff reductions.

The Tufts to Parkend section of the line was to be singled, Whitecroft box being removed, and the signal box at Upper Lydbrook was also to be closed. It was also proposed to single the line between Sharpness South and Berkeley Road, a distance of some 3 miles. Misgiving was expressed at the effect of this on the ability to take trains diverted because of accident or repair work from the Severn Tunnel route, but it was considered that the existing 2½ mile single line section from Otters Pool Junction to Severn Bridge was already the limiting factor in arranging train diversions between Lydney and Berkeley Road.

The possibility of using auto or Sentinel steam railcars between Lydney and Berkeley Road was also considered but it was pointed out that they would not be as economical as engines which could be used for both passenger and freight trains.

The handling and storage of colliery empties was another cause for concern. A meeting on 28th February 1929 revealed that an increase of coal traffic, from 2000 to 4000 tons a day, was necessitating the outstabling of empty wagons on the Lydney and Sharpness dock lines. The accommodation at Lydney yard was inadequate and, because of the congestion, the GW 'down' refuge siding was frequently blocked when the exchange roads were full. It was the only refuge siding for 'up' or 'down' freight trains between Bullo Pill and Portskewett and the loss of this facility meant that main line trains were either delayed waiting acceptance at Lydney or were shunted from one running line to another for passenger trains to pass.

The problem arose from:

1. Inadequate siding accommodation at some of the collieries to cope with all of the wagons sent to them by coal factors and other merchants in addition to their own, the latter being used mainly between the collieries and the docks. (The last empties for the collieries left Lydney at 3.50 p.m., but if the collieries could accommodate them a special train of empties was sometimes run between 6.00 and 7.00 p.m.)

2. Inadequate accommodation at Lydney Junction S & W except when there was a depression in the coal trade.

3. Frequent staff changes by the LMS whose men were unfamiliar with the geography of the line or the districts to which the coal was consigned.

It was decided that additional sidings were needed at Princess Royal, Mierystock and Cannop. Accommodation at the latter was designed for a daily output of 400 tons while the output at the time had increased from 1000 to 4000 tons per week.

Extra siding accommodation was also suggested at Lydney Junction S & W where alterations to three sidings would give space for an extra fifty wagons to facilitate exchange with the GW.

Until extra accommodation could be arranged, it was decided that whenever there was room at Lydney docks, coal empties should be worked there from Lydney Junction joint yard during the evening to leave room to accept 100 wagons from the GWR during the night. Sharpness was also to be used when necessary in connection with empties from the West of England.

It was pointed out that this would involve extra engine power and Lydney docks was not a very suitable place to put the wagons.

A further report of 9th March 1929 suggested that when the 'down' line between Tufts and Parkend was taken out of use between Tufts and Whitecroft, it should be retained as a storage siding for about 100 wagons.

The same report also included a proposal from the Gloucester Divisional Superintendent that the neighbouring Great Western railmotor service between Newnham, Bilson, Cinderford and Drybrook be replaced by road buses, but this was not taken any further.

With the proposed economies being agreed, the officers of the Joint Committee made an official inspection of the line. This appears to have been a most agreeable tour, a special eight-wheeled inspection saloon leaving Gloucester on Monday, 6th May, at 10.50 a.m. complete with 'two dozen luncheon baskets to be put into the coach, also one dozen bottles of Bass and two bottles of ginger ale'!

At a subsequent meeting on 12th June, it was decided to withdraw the passenger services from 8th July, the last trains running on Saturday 6th, but the Sharpness South to Berkeley Road singling was deferred. Passengers were to be served by the existing bus operations as these were felt to be adequate and the area too sparsely populated to support railway buses in addition.

The *Dean Forest Mercury* for Friday, 14th June, carried news of the impending closure but in concluding under the heading 'PUBLIC OPINION CALM' said 'It is not anticipated that there will be any outburst of public indignation at the Company's decision. The truth is that the passenger railway service has not entered very fully into the life of the Forest, and since the 'buses have developed their splendid cross country and co-related services the railway line has been more and more neglected.' However, whether this was true or not, the bias of the article is betrayed by the following remark, 'We have not compared the fares: probably these also are in favour of the road vehicle.' (!)

The *Western Mail & South Wales News* for Tuesday, 18th June, took quite a different stand and reported strong protests by the Coleford and District Improvement Association. Many of the members were trying to popularize the Forest and turn it into a National Park and the railway company were giving them a serious setback, 'One of the heaviest blows Coleford had ever had'. The paper also stated that during the winter 'buses are sometimes held up for two or three days, and in one instance the Forest buses were held up for ten days'.

Mr. D. J. Vaughan, M.P. for the Forest of Dean, spent 2½ hours at a meeting on the evening of Saturday 22nd discussing with a deputation the question of the train services being withdrawn and also making the Forest a National Park. Afterwards he immediately wrote to the GWR and Ministry of Transport appealing for proposals to be suspended until the local authorities had been able to enquire into the matter.

On 27th June *The Citizen* made further mention of the matter, their Lydney correspondent claiming that there would be no inconvenience to the local community as it was understood on good authority that both Red & White Services and Bristol Tramways Co. would be filling up any necessary gaps.

The Royal Forest of Dean Association and the Coleford & District Improvement Association, backed by the Wye Valley Development Association and Coleford Urban Council, protested to the companies, but Vaughan's reply from Sir Felix Pole (General Manager of the GWR) pointed out 'The companies were faced with the fact that the maintenance of these services involves a heavy financial loss, and it is evident from the small number of passengers using the trains there is no longer any real public demand for the services.'

A deputation from the Forest attended a meeting at Paddington on Wednesday afternoon, 3rd July, and for 1½ hours they endeavoured to dissuade the officials of the GWR from their decision.

It transpired that during May not one passenger train in or out of Coleford had carried a dozen passengers. The first train out in the morning during one week had two passengers on Monday, none on Wednesday and one on each of the other mornings. The 9.03 a.m. 'which might be expected to carry scholars and others' averaged eight passengers a day and another train averaged six. In fact the only train which reached double figures was about 5.00 p.m. and that averaged eleven.

The local people were simply not using the railway and, not surprisingly, the passenger services were withdrawn as scheduled. The parcels and goods services were continued by road, a 30 cwt. Thornycroft, which com-

The last regular passenger train at Coleford on Saturday, 6th June 1929. *Collection A. K. Pope*

menced on 8th July, being based at Coleford, where the existing agreement with a cartage agent for parcels traffic was terminated on 1st December that year, the agent continuing to handle goods traffic.

Upper Lydbrook signal box was taken out of use on 8th October and the electric train staff working from Serridge to Lydbrook Junction was replaced by a wooden train staff. However, the singling of the line between Tufts and Parkend was deferred because of increasing coal traffic and the question of its retention was discussed at a committee meeting on 23rd October.

It seems that despite the withdrawal of passenger services, delays were still occurring which were attributed to the following: At Tufts no trains could be accepted from Whitecroft or Lydney Town while a train was running from Moseley Green on the Mineral Loop, nor was any train allowed to leave Moseley when one had been accepted from Whitecroft or Lydney. The running time from Moseley Green to Tufts was approximately 25 minutes down a 1 in 40 gradient. Delays were also experienced at Tufts waiting acceptance from Lydney Town and, because of restrictions governing the use of the third or mineral line between 6.00 a.m. and 11.00 a.m., the general working was interfered with. This was remedied in the first instance by the surely long overdue provision of a sand drag at the end of the Mineral Loop line at Tufts Junction, which enabled the associated restrictions to be lifted.

The third line between Lydney and Lydney Town was authorized for use when required and because of the increased traffic some of the trains were re-timed whilst other aspects of operation were also reviewed.

The 'down' main line was subsequently taken out of use between Tufts and Parkend on Sunday, 30th November 1930, an electric train staff system being introduced on this section, whilst the double line between Parkend and Coleford Junction was retained. Whitecroft signal box was also taken out of use and, whilst the 'down' line between Parkend and Whitecroft was recovered, the stretch between Whitecroft and Tufts was retained for use as a siding.

The motor economic system of maintenance had also been introduced north of Coleford Junction (including the Coleford branch and mineral loop) on 26th June 1930.

With the restrictions and timekeeping associated with providing a passenger service now over, the Severn & Wye settled into a new era with freedom to concentrate on the more lucrative mineral traffic. The network of rails leading through the Forest, scattered with occasional stray sheep, must have given the impression of forgotten and even lonely byways. However, this was far from the case for, despite the peace and beauty of the surroundings, the well worn rail tops were kept bright and shiny from the passage of the Lydney pannier tanks barking to and fro with seemingly endless trains of multi-coloured wagons serving the many and varied local industries scattered throughout the area.

The local motor bus services were run by the Red & White Bus Co. in conjunction with the Bristol Tramways Co., but while the traffic during the week was regarded

Cinderford Junction on 28th September 1946 displaying a fine selection of GWR wooden post signals. The original extension line from Drybrook Road station disappears into the middle distance, whilst the later GWR line connecting Cinderford with the Forest of Dean branch curves away to the left towards Bilson Junction.   *L. E. Copeland*

as fairly light, the hourly service on Saturdays was inadequate to cope with the growing needs of the local people. In September 1932 a meeting was held to consider the partial restoration of passenger services between

A ganger with one of the motorized trolleys at Cinderford Junction, probably soon after the introduction of the Motor Economic System of Maintenance. In brief, the system allowed the ganger total occupation of a section of line through the possession of an occupation key which had to be replaced at a mid section instrument (or signal box) before the signalman could withdraw the train token. This avoided the need for flagmen who were otherwise posted in advance of the work in either direction.
Collection A. K. Pope

Lydney Town and Parkend on Saturdays only, but nothing came of this.

During the following month, the economy of working the Lydney to Berkeley services by an 'oil unit' was also considered. However, whilst the 'oil unit' was rejected because of the difficulties in strengthening the service with tail loads over a 1 in 132 gradient, it was recommended that auto trailers could be employed. These could be worked on the branch without a guard except for the 8.22 a.m. Berkeley to Lydney and the 4.15 p.m. Lydney to Berkeley trains, which it was felt needed a guard to ensure the safety of the 60 or so school children travelling to school at Lydney each day.

The existing services were operated with four LMS bogie coaches and six GW 4-wheeled vehicles, half of each being used on alternate days while the others were being cleaned. By providing just three 60 ft auto trailers instead, one on regular services, one for the schools trains and one spare for cleaning and strengthening purposes, it was possible to effect an economy in engine power of 2½ hours each day and enable two guards to be dispensed with. In the absence of the guard, the station staff would be responsible for supervising the departure of each train, but in their absence the fireman would assume these responsibilities.

The auto trailers were eventually provided but not until 30th November 1936, Lydney shed consequently being provided with auto fitted GWR Collett 0—4—2Ts to work them as push and pull units.

During the Second World War, as with similar areas of wooded cover, the Forest of Dean was used for the storage of explosives and ammunition. Both Hawthorns tunnel on the Great Western's Forest of Dean branch and Moseley tunnel on the Severn & Wye Mineral Loop were requi-

GWR '2021' class pannier tank No. 2043 passing through Lydney Town station in later years, and signalled for the third line to Lydney Junction, on one of the many mineral workings which were the mainstay of Severn & Wye services. *W. A. Camwell*

No. 2080 at Lydney Town with the 8.00 p.m. auto train to Berkeley Road on 9th August 1947. *W. A. Camwell*

sitioned by the military for ammunition stores, while No. 28 ASD Cinderford had depots at Acorn Patch, again on the Mineral Loop, Speech House Road and Parkend.

The Mineral Loop was broken between Moseley tunnel and New Fancy colliery on 15th May 1942, ammunition trains being propelled to the tunnel from Tufts Junction. However, the Acorn Patch depot, brought into use on 9th March 1943, apparently acquired strategic importance with some 80 wagons in and out each day. It was situated on the northern section of the Mineral Loop midway between New Fancy and Drybrook Road but the needs of the military could not be met with the existing arrangements so the Moseley tunnel store was abandoned, the missing track reinstated and the loop restored on 29th December 1943. The shorter route via Tufts Junction was a great improvement but at a meeting on 31st December a GWR representative stated that 'it would be wise now to anticipate that the urgency of the next few months, or even weeks, might force the army authorities to make demands for shunting at any of the three depots, or for special trips, with well nigh no previous notice.' After hearing that the existing 'engine power is fully absorbed'

the meeting concluded that in order to cover round the clock working, an additional engine, 7 sets of enginemen and 7 guards would be required (another 3 guards were also needed on top of this as they were already below the normal allocation). The outcome is not recorded but crews recall the depot being in use for 24 hours a day, and some of them were certainly called out again after their own shifts from which they were so often late home at this time. The depot was not closed until 1949.

The wartime operations had brought extra traffic to the line which in part replaced the lost colliery output. In fact the Mineral Loop was able to be used for military needs because it had lost virtually all its coal traffic. Crump Meadow Colliery had closed in 1929, followed by Foxes Bridge Colliery in 1931. Lightmoor Colliery closed in 1940 leaving only New Fancy Colliery, which at this time had an output of only about 12 wagons a fortnight and was served from Drybrook Road. The closure of New Fancy in 1944 left the military depot as the only reason for retaining the Mineral Loop.

The contraction of the system following further colliery closures will be described in a subsequent volume.

Motor-fitted '2021' class 0—6—0PT No. 2080 at Berkeley Road on the 6.35 p.m. to Lydney on 9th August 1947.
                                                                    W. A. Camwell

CHAPTER FIVE

ALONG THE LINE

An early view of the Great Western station at Lydney Junction, looking towards Chepstow. The Severn & Wye carriage shed is visible beyond the nearest telegraph pole, the unusual shape betraying its former use as a church. *Collection Neil Parkhouse*

LYDNEY JUNCTION

The layout at Lydney Junction evolved primarily for the exchange of wagons with the Great Western and for the sorting of wagons to and from the docks. The original S & W station was a terminus situated at right angles to the GWR South Wales main line adjacent to the docks line. It had a single platform with two faces and a simple timber-built booking office provided by Messrs. William Eassie & Co. Ltd. of Gloucester in 1874, about a year before the line was opened for passenger traffic. The track plan is featured on page 35.

In 1879 the first station was superseded by another situated on the new curve connecting the Severn & Wye and Severn Bridge Railways. It was reached by means of a long footbridge which, commencing behind the GWR station, provided a direct connection between the two companies. It spanned the existing exchange sidings, but with economy ever to the fore, extended only as far as the southernmost platform, the two platforms themselves being connected only by means of boarded crossings. The main building, situated on the 'down' platform, was built by the Gloucester Wagon Company, Messrs. Eassie & Co's successors, and incorporated the building from the original station. The shelter on the 'up' platform was also provided by them.

In 1880 an 'iron church' from Cheltenham was purchased for £150 and intended for use as a 'carriage and locomotive shed and workshop'. It measured 133 ft x 70 ft and, complete with at least some of its stained glass windows, was re-erected alongside the former terminus spanning five tracks as shown on the track plan. In practice, it seems to have been used as a carriage shed with only the occasional loco being stored there, but it was not until 1897 that stop blocks were provided at the end of each siding when it had been brought to the Joint Committee's attention that there were 'no effective appliances for preventing vehicles running off the rails'. The picture at the head of the page is the only view discovered so far showing this elusive corrugated iron structure. It is not clear whether the shed was simply not large enough or inconveniently situated, but in 1899 'a siding' holding 5 coaches was extended as the coal roads, which were always at a premium, were evidently also being used for passenger vehicles. Extensive repairs were carried out to the shed in 1904 at a cost of £145 but it was removed in 1924 when the sidings were utilized for much needed sorting accommodation. A full time carriage cleaner had been based here at one time and the shed had also been used as a paint shop.

In 1899 it is recorded that 157 men were engaged at Lydney Junction which gives some idea of the activity there. However, this fact came to light in a complaint from the employees in which it was pointed out that there was no 'latrine accommodation' for the staff. Presumably the gents lavatory at the station was in frequent demand. The only staff mess was a small building over the loco work-shops where the men had their meals and which, besides

Another view of the GWR station, looking west along the South Wales main line on 10th April 1948. This crossed the Severn & Wye line to the harbour by means of a right-angled level crossing immediately beyond the end of the platforms (see page 49). The water tower on the left belonged to the GWR and was quite independent of the S & W supply.   *L. E. Copeland*

An early 1960s view of the ex-South Wales Railway station taken from the S & W crossing. The water column between the running lines is prominent, and the more easterly of the two wagon repair buildings may just be seen beyond this. The distinctive station nameboard is the complement of that on the Severn & Wye station, reading 'Lydney change for Severn & Wye Joint Railway'. A thriving passenger traffic to London from here was apparently well established even before the Severn & Wye passenger services commenced, as a memorial from the inhabitants of Lydney in 1873 complains of the inconvenience caused by the evening express from Paddington no longer stopping at the station. The same letter also requested an increase in the number or power of the station lights.   *Lens of Sutton*

A complementary picture to that on the facing page, looking in the opposite direction from the top of the same signal, with the Great Western cattle pens in the foreground and the Severn & Wye lines to the far left. Lydney Junction signal box can be seen in the middle distance.

L. E. Copeland

suffering from difficult access, was apparently devoid of lockers, etc. Also hand and carriage lamps were trimmed outside as there were no proper facilities. The staff consequently requested an improved mess room, lamp room, latrine accommodation and improved lighting in the shunting sidings. The request was approved without hesitation, an estimated £340 being sanctioned for the necessary accommodation, including four 3-burner lamps in the yard. Later improvements included a mess room for loco men and an additional store for the lineman, both provided in 1908.

The complex of sidings predictably evolved with the passing of time according to traffic requirements. In 1886 £1,000 was authorized for the provision of 'additional sidings at Lydney Junction and docks' employing serviceable iron rails and chairs from relaying the Coleford branch. It appears that the work was not finished until August 1890 when it was reported that the re-arrangement and signalling of the transfer and marshalling sidings was complete. A further £1,430 authorized in 1910 appears to have been for the three 'Severn Bridge Sidings', which extended from behind the S & W station alongside the existing sidings to

terminate short of Lydney Junction signal box. They became known as Severn Bridge Nos. 3, 4 and 5 and must have been a great help in relieving congestion. However, space was always at a premium and, during the accommodation problems in 1929 discussed in chapter 3, the eastern end of the original Severn Bridge sidings were also extended to alleviate the problems caused by excess numbers of colliery empties.

In 1928 the staff at Lydney Junction under District Inspector Bracey were as follows: a district inspector class 4, 3 yard foreman class 1, 3 shunters class 1, 5 shunters class 3 (two of which worked in the docks), 29 goods guards (9 turns of duty requiring 2 guards), and 3 number takers, the night shift man working the yard 'box from 10.00 p.m. until relieved by the engine shed 'box signalman, and again between 4.00 a.m. and 6.00 a.m.

The Junction station was staffed by a porter signalman, who was employed in Otters Pool Junction signal box from 12 noon to 3.00 p.m., and a class 2 porter, the station coming under the supervision of the Lydney GW station master.

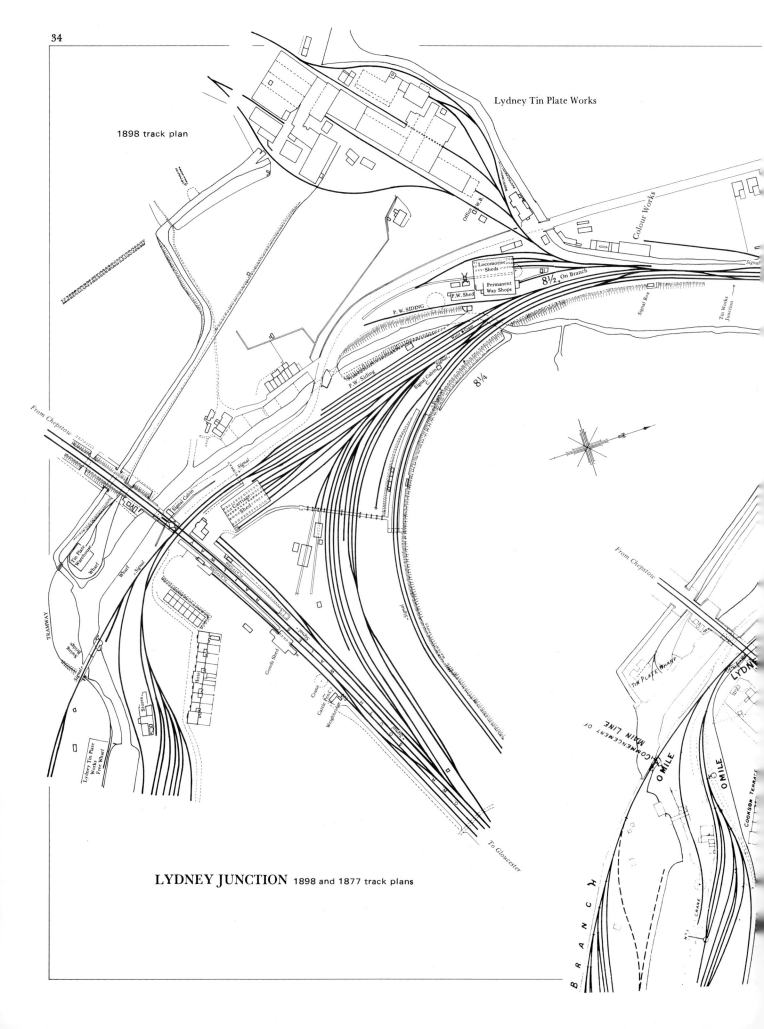

34

Lydney Tin Plate Works

1898 track plan

Colour Works

Locomotive Sheds

Permanent Way Shops

P.W. Shed

8½ On Branch

Signal Box

Tin Works Junction

P. W. SIDING

P. W. SIDING

8¼

From Chepstow

Signal

Signal Cabin

Signal Cabin C

Signal

Carriage Shed

Tin Plate Warehouse

Wharf

Wharf

Signal

TRAMWAY

Swing Bridge

Signal

Stores

Hotel

Goods Shed

Crane

Cattle Pens

Weighbridge

Lydney Tin Plate Works Free Wharf

From Chepstow

TIN PLATE WHARF

COMMENCEMENT OF MAIN LINE

LYDNEY

0 MILE

0 MILE

COOKSON TERRACE

BRANCH

CRANE

No 1

To Gloucester

LYDNEY JUNCTION 1898 and 1877 track plans

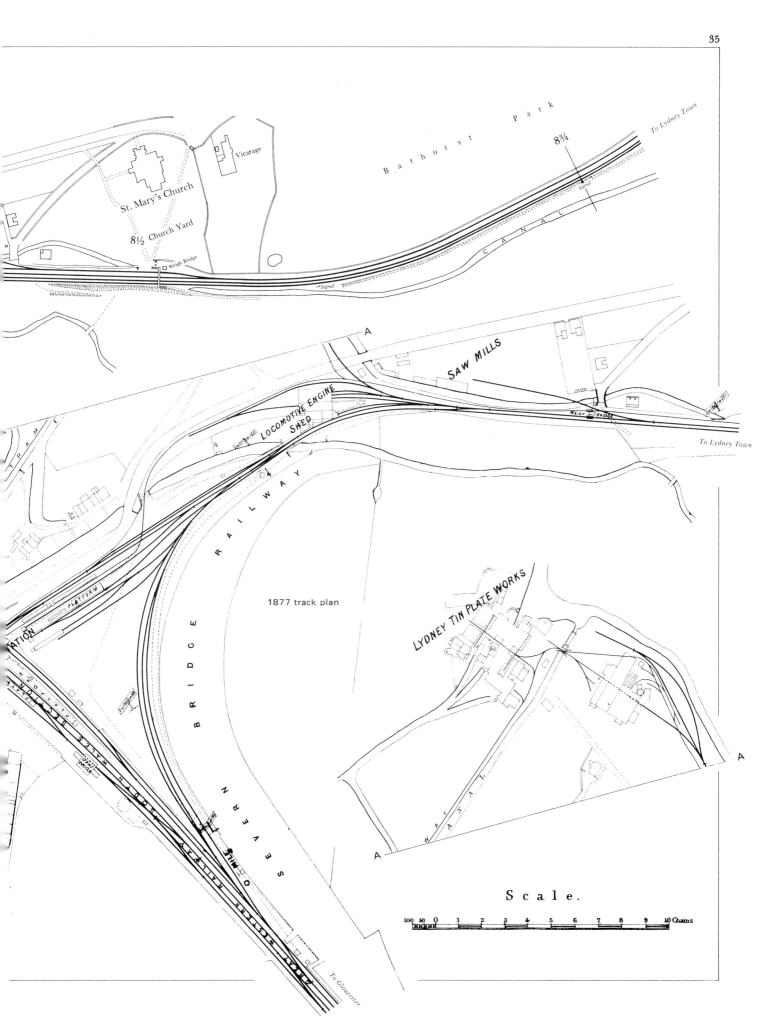

Bathurst Park

To Lydney Town

8¾

Signal

C A N A L

Vicarage

St. Mary's Church

8½ Church Yard

Weigh Bridge

Signal

A

SAW MILLS

WEIGH BRIDGE

To Lydney Town

LOCOMOTIVE ENGINE SHED

T R A M

R A I L W A Y

B R I D G E

1877 track plan

PLATFORM

STATION

S E V E R N

8 MILE

SOUTH WALES RAILWAY

PLATFORM

LYDNEY TIN PLATE WORKS

C A N A L

A

A

A

To Gloucester

S c a l e .

100 50 0 1 2 3 4 5 6 7 8 9 10 Chains

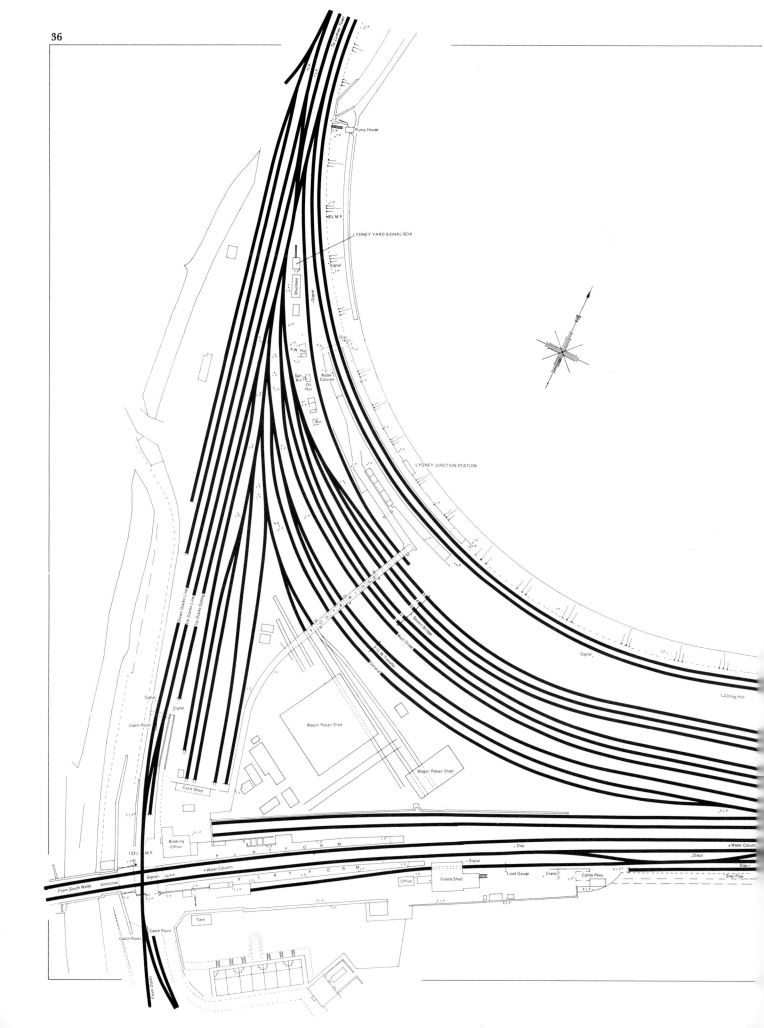

To Lydney Town

Pump House

8¼ M.P.

LYDNEY YARD SIGNAL BOX

Signal

Shunters

Signal

P.W. Hut

Disc

Salt Bin

Oil Hut

Water Column

Bin

LYDNEY JUNCTION STATION

Down Docks Line

Up Docks Line

Up Docks Siding

FOOT BRIDGE

Severn Bridge

Not Order

P.W. Transit

General

Signal

Fog Hut

Signal

Signal

Catch Point

Wagon Repair Shed

Wagon Repair Shed

Cycle Shed

Booking Office

133¾ M.P.

PLATFORM

Water Column

Signal

Water Column

Discs

Disc

From South Wales

PLATFORM

Disc

Office

Goods Shed

Load Gauge

Crane

Cattle Pens

Stay Pole

Tank

Catch Point

Catch Point

From Docks

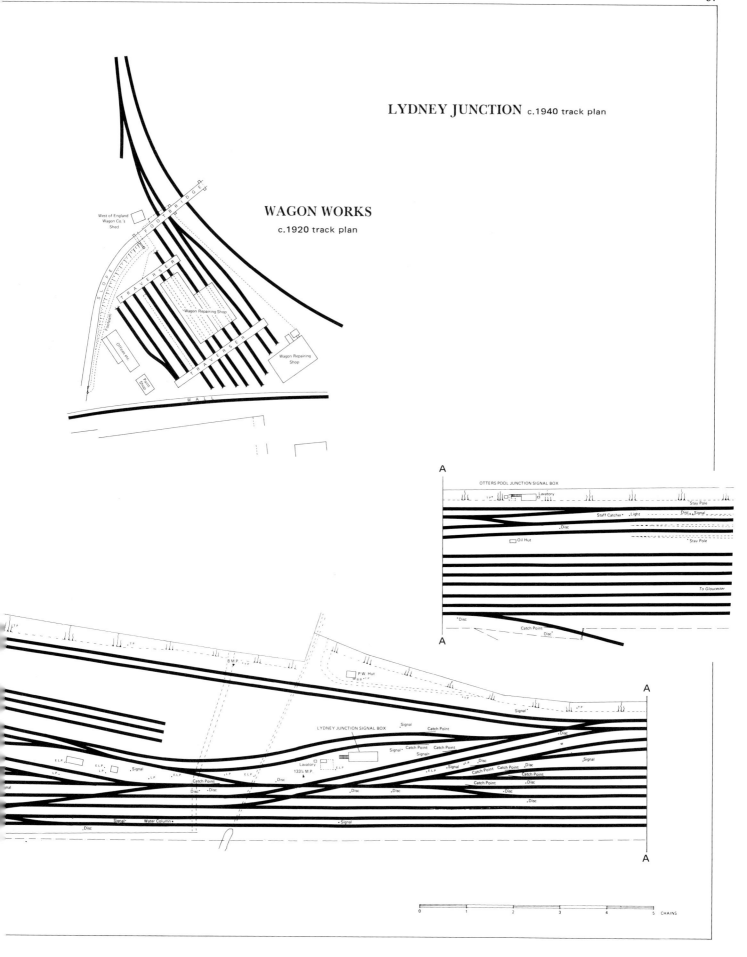

LYDNEY JUNCTION c.1940 track plan

WAGON WORKS

c.1920 track plan

West of England
Wagon Co.'s
Shed

FOOTBRIDGE

SLOPE

TRAVERSER

Footpath

Wagon Repairing Shop

Office etc.

Point Shed

TRAVERSER

Wagon Repairing
Shop

WALL

OTTERS POOL JUNCTION SIGNAL BOX

Lavatory

Stay Pole

Staff Catcher   Light

Disc   Signal

Disc

Oil Hut

Stay Pole

To Gloucester

Disc

Catch Point

Disc

B.M.P.

P.W. Hut

LYDNEY JUNCTION SIGNAL BOX

Signal

Catch Point

Signal

Disc

Signal   Catch Point   Catch Point

Lavatory

133¾ M.P.

Signal

Catch Point   Signal

E.L.P.   Disc

Signal   Disc

E.L.P.
L.P.   Signal

Catch Point   Catch Point

Disc

Catch Point   Disc

L.P.   Catch Point

Disc   Disc

Catch Point

Disc

Disc

Disc   Disc

Signal   Water Column

Signal

Disc

0   1   2   3   4   5 CHAINS

A closer view of the junctions between the GWR and former Severn & Wye and Severn Bridge Railway, again on 10th April 1948. The running crossovers from the main line provide access to and from the single line to Berkeley (over the Severn Bridge), the other end of these being worked by Otters Pool Junction signal box. The junction was sanctioned for use by the Board of Trade on 30th August 1879, when the Severn Bridge Railway was still nominally an independent undertaking, although plans for amalgamation with the Severn & Wye were well advanced. The lines behind the signal box led into the Severn Bridge exchange sidings behind the S & W station. The two buildings in the foreground belonged to the GWR. The larger was a PW Dept. stores and mess while the other was the GW yard foreman's office. The shed next to the signal box served as an oil hut.

L. E. Copeland

The original Lydney Junction box supplied by the Gloucester Wagon Co. in 1880.   *GRC & W Co.*

Returning to the GWR main line now, this picture taken on 20th April 1933 shows the throat of the GW exchange sidings. These were used for the transfer of traffic between the main line and the Forest. Before the opening of the Severn Bridge Railway, this had been the only connection between the two companies. At this date the crossover between the goods shed and exchange sidings road was connected to the 'down' running line by a single slip, later altered to a double slip as shown opposite. *L. E. Copeland*

A closer view of Lydney Junction signal box. This was a timber structure built in 1904 to a standard GWR design, replacing the one illustrated opposite. Expenses appertaining to both the crossing and junction boxes had been shared equally between the two companies, but from about 1903 they were split on a leverage principle, between the GW and the S & W. The cost of the new box, estimated at £1,491, was also shared on this principle. *L. E. Copeland*

Access to the S & W station was provided by means of an extensive lattice iron footbridge which spanned the exchange sidings, gentle approach ramps at either end enabling luggage and parcels to be ferried to and from the platforms on trolleys. This structure dated from 1908 when, at a cost of some £2,700, it replaced a simpler structure (with steps) as featured on the track plan on page 34. For transferring passengers' luggage, etc. from the GW station to their original terminus, the Severn & Wye, in September 1875, paid the Great Western £60 per annum. With the old station this presented little difficulty. However, with the formation of the Joint Committee, the GW discovered that it had been performing the much longer haul to the new station over the footbridge under the same agreement and at the same cost! By this time the traffic also included twenty or so milk churns each day *en route* from Berkeley to South Wales. *R. Marrows*

Looking east along the Severn Bridge line with Otters Pool Junction signal box on the left. This and the signal in the foreground were standard MR designs provided in late 1914 after that company had taken over responsibility for the line from Berkeley to Coleford Junction. The fourth line from the left is the siding that was made into the 'down' goods line in 1941. *L. E. Copeland*

A GWR Collett 0–4–2T approaching the S & W station with an auto train from Berkeley Road on 10th April 1948.   *L. E. Copeland*

The Severn & Wye and Severn Bridge Railway station on 26th June 1948. While the station building had the appearance of a standard Gloucester Wagon Co. structure (similar to those later provided on the Golden Valley Railway), it incorporated the smaller William Eassie structure from the original terminus. This had measured some 20 ft x 9 ft 6 ins x 10 ft high 'at the sides'. The rebuilt version incorporated a new general waiting room, 16 ft x 7 ft 9 ins, a ladies waiting room (with W.C.) 10 ft x 7 ft 9 ins, urinals and a coal house. The building was constructed of red deal clad with 'rusticated weatherboarding' and lined with ¾ inch matched boarding. The roof was covered with best Countess slates and finished with ornamental ridge tiling and 4 inch OG cast guttering with 2½ inch downpipes. The shelter on the opposite platform was a standard Gloucester Wagon Co. structure.   *L. E. Copeland*

Another view of the Gloucester Wagon Co. station building dwarfed by the incongruous sloping ramp of the lattice footbridge. The large nameboard was provided in 1898, the Joint Committee having decided that one reading 'Lydney Junction change for South Wales, Paddington and the Great Western Line', should be provided at a cost of £9 10s 0d. The one alongside was one of four provided by the LMS. The Midland style station fencing may have been provided when the footbridge was replaced. From 1923 the GW and S & W stations were linked with 'telephone communication' to 'assist in arrangements in connection with the running of trains, especially when running out of course'.
L. E. Copeland

This two lever ground frame, photographed in July 1947, was situated on the 'down' platform alongside the station building. It was provided to meet the Board of Trade requirement whereby passenger trains standing in stations had to be protected by fixed signals. If there was no signal box at the station, as in the case of Lydney Junction, a lever frame to return the home and distant signals to danger had to be provided. Such frames were operated by the platform staff or, in their absence, the guard. Subsequently, when the use of halts became more common, the Board of Trade waived the rule and by the 1930s platform levers became a rarity.

Here at Lydney Junction only one of the levers on the 'down' platform was in use. It worked a slot on the Otters Pool down starting signal (effectively the Lydney Junction station home). The distant signal in this case was fixed so did not require a lever although, as can be seen, a spare was provided.

On the 'up' platform both levers were in use, one working the home (Engine Shed box up starting signal) and distant (see diagram on page 61). Both lever frames were taken out of use in 1954.
L. E. Copeland

An undated view looking south-east through the station, showing the foot of the access ramp.

Lens of Sutton

The passengers' view from the footbridge approach ramp with a 'down' train being watered in the platform before completing its journey to Lydney Town on 2nd July 1947. Locos on the Berkeley auto service had to take water here as there was no crane alongside the opposite platform and no supply at all at the town station. A similar water crane was also provided at Coleford.

L. E. Copeland

Another view looking towards Lydney Town with an auto train for Berkeley approaching the platform on 10th April 1948. The Midland's presence is very much in evidence here with that company's trespass boards, fencing, lamps, signals and signal box. The plain brick building behind the train was the 1899 mess room for the yard staff and guards. It also incorporated the S & W yard foreman's office in the end nearest the signal box. The grounded van body is believed to have also been provided in 1899 for use as a lamp hut. The Midland later provided two of their standard corrugated iron lamp huts alongside, one of which is shown on the left. The River Lyd was bridged alongside the engine shed, the corrugated iron pump house just visible on the right of the nameboard, being situated on the river bank alongside one of the wing walls. The original backing signal at the end of the platform was provided in 1923, at a cost of £30 6s. 9d., to control the movement of trains setting back to Engine Shed Junction for disposal in the sidings. The elevated disc shown here is a later replacement.

L. E. Copeland

WAGON REPAIR SIDINGS

With the large numbers of wagons being handled, some of which could spend much of their time travelling between a single colliery and the docks, there were always wagons in need of attention. As a result the junction became the site of various wagon repair establishments at different times, particularly in the triangular plot between the carriage shed and the two stations. Some of the details are not at all clear but in 1889 Joseph Boucher, trading as the Forest of Dean Wagon Co., occupied an unspecified plot, and from 1891 the North Central Wagon Co. leased 100 square yards of land for the purpose of building an office and repair hut. Whether either of these companies had their own siding is not known. The Standard Wagon Co. occupied a siding running south through the footbridge and were joined in 1897 by the Gloucester Railway Carriage and Wagon Co. who had previously occupied another site somewhere in the yard from 1889. The connection for the GRC & W Co.'s new siding, to which they apparently moved their repair shed, effectively reduced the length of the Standard Wagon Co.'s siding by about 78 ft so a corresponding extension was made at the opposite end at the expense of the GRC & W. The Standard Wagon Co. took the opportunity of having another 50 ft of track added at the same time. Their tenancy was taken over by the Albion Carriage Co. Ltd. in 1902 and in turn their interests were acquired by the British Wagon Co. Ltd. in 1903. The British Wagon Co. were in 1909 authorized to construct an additional siding on their site which occupied an area of approximately 304 square yards.

In 1901 Messrs. Hurst Nelson & Co. Ltd. rented a repairing hut and an area of land beside the siding alongside the carriage shed. Their agreement also allowed them to stand trucks for repairing purposes on the sidings at a toll of 6d per wagon per week. In 1920 a hut on virtually the same site was taken over by the West of England Wagon Co. until their removal in 1925 to a siding between the engine shed and Lydney church. The British Wagon Co. and the GRC & W, however, remained until about 1922 when it appears that the whole site was taken over by Wagon Repairs Ltd. who enlarged the works between 1922 and 1926. The works closed in 1964.

Looking south-east over the junction sidings from the station footbridge on 10th April 1948. Two of the three lines curving through the centre of the picture were used for the transfer of traffic to and from the Forest via the Severn Bridge route and were known as Severn Bridge sidings 2 and 1 respectively. The third was used for wait order coal. The three sidings to the left, terminating in the distance, were known as Severn Bridge Nos. 3-5 and used to hold some of the huge numbers of empties until required. Trains of these vehicles were usually made up on one of the through roads. The three lines to the right were used for the exchange of traffic with the GWR. *L. E. Copeland*

The long span of the footbridge mainly obscures one of the few views discovered of the wagon repair works. *R. Marrows*

A 1960s view showing the full extent of the lengthy footbridge connecting the two stations. *R. Marrows*

Another view from the footbridge, this time looking north-west on 2nd July 1947. The S & W station is on the right with the engine shed centre distant. The crane to the left of the shed belonged to the PW Dept. which had a siding on either side of the river. The tinplate works, on the opposite side of Church Road, are also featured on the left. The siding behind the S & W station had been extended, possibly in 1915, and was used as alternative storage for coaching stock, the carriage shed apparently often being congested. *L. E. Copeland*

Looking south along the two docks lines leading to the harbour on 10th April 1948, with Lydney Yard signal box on the left. Each of the two daytime shifts was manned by a full time signalman who operated the points for the sorting and exchange sidings. They received instructions from the shunter who shouted out the numbers of each siding required while splitting off wagons throughout the lengthy shunting operations. The sidings on the right were used for empties from the harbour. *L. E. Copeland*

A '54XX' hauled auto train passing behind Lydney Yard box on its way to Lydney Town in 1947. *W. A. Camwell*

48

The view south from the yard box on 10th April 1948 with the South Wales main line and crossing box on the horizon. The original S & W terminus was situated alongside the lines to the harbour while the carriage shed had straddled the sidings on the left. *L. E. Copeland*

Lydney Yard box was another Midland structure believed to have been provided in 1919 to supplement the new Lydney Engine Shed box, the latter controlling most of the junctions and all signalling on the running lines. The yard box had the sole function of operating the pointwork for the station and yard sidings. As part of the improvements, the yard points now operated by this box were altered so as to be detected by the signals controlling movements in and out of the station siding, which were operated by the Engine Shed box (confirmed as completed 19th January 1920). It is shown here on 20th April 1933. *L. E. Copeland*

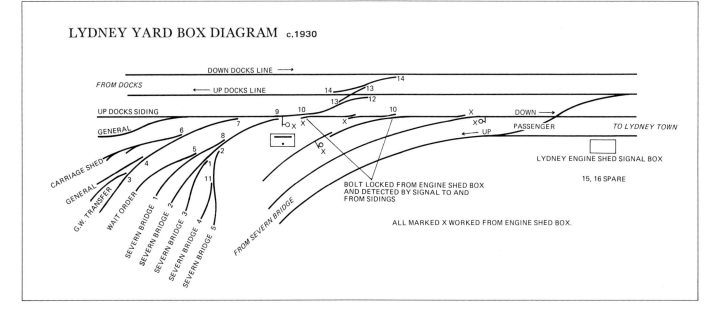

LYDNEY YARD BOX DIAGRAM c.1930

A closer view of the rear of the GWR station, one of the entrances to which had latterly been via a subway beneath the S & W to the path on the left. This had formerly provided access to the original S & W terminus. The crossing leading to the docks was controlled by the GWR Lydney West signal box and was the source of ill feeling between the two companies when in 1878 the Great Western revised the arrangements without consulting the Severn & Wye. As soon as they realized that the revision left them at a disadvantage, the S & W complained to the Board of Trade claiming that the level crossing was theirs as it was the GWR who had crossed their line when they opened the South Wales main line in 1851. They objected 'on the ground (amongst others) that they are calculated to impede our traffic on its way to and from the Docks of our Company'. The Great Western admitted the difference of opinion between the two companies 'as to the desirability of interlocking the crossing gates with the signals and also with regard to providing catchpoints on their line.' Grierson of the GWR went on 'I scarcely need to say that what we propose to do is solely with a view to prevent the possibility of an accident at the crossing and not as might be inferred from Mr. Keeling's letter impede S & W Co.'s traffic to and from their Docks and to otherwise injure their property.'

The S & W particularly objected to the safety points and felt they 'could continually endanger our engine and trucks getting off the line — They would also limit our standing room for trains formed for the morning.' They also objected to the interlocking of newly erected gates which were intended to prevent trespass on the GWR, all of this preventing the hitherto practice of light engines being hand signalled over the crossing without moving the signals, 'by which much time is saved in shunting'. In stating their case, the S & W feared the delays waiting for the crossing which was controlled by a Great Western Company's servant who 'would naturally be anxious to avoid going through the routine several times of moving all signals and opening or closing gates'. Keeling further pleaded 'it is of vital importance to have the communication over the crossing to the docks as free as possible — The Great Western Co. are a large and powerful Company and the Severn and Wye Co. a very weak one'.

At the time a tramroad line crossed the GWR alongside the 4' 8½" track of the S & W and what at the time was described as a cart track. In an attempt to resolve the problems, the Board of Trade stipulated that catchpoints south of the crossing were to be situated between 16 and 20 yards from it and those to the north at 12 yards. A pair of point rails was to be provided in each case, the outside switch being 'covered with about 8 to 12 inches of sand boxed to form a dead end so that an engine or waggon which may slightly overrun the safety points shall not drop off the rails unless it runs further than the switch rail which should be about 16 ft long'. Block working was also stipulated on the main line to avoid delays. This was already in operation between Lydney and Awre Jcn. to the east and was introduced between Lydney and Woolaston, to the west, on 1st September 1879.

The arrangements were controlled from a new signal box, built at the end of 1878, with a 20 lever frame (6 spare), 2 bolt locking levers, and wheel apparatus for opening and closing the crossing gates. The frame was evidently later extended, as in 1903, when the expenses for the crossing box were split on a leverage basis, the GW bore 11/28 of the expense. The timber built signal box featured here (a standard GWR design) replaced the one discussed in 1916.

The spur on the left remained from the second ('up docks') line which formerly crossed the GW. This was truncated in 1908. All trains to the harbour were propelled over the crossing but the harbour itself is described in a subsequent volume. This picture was taken on 6th September 1947.   L. E. Copeland

A later view looking back from the crossing on 17th August 1956, again showing the site of the original terminus. The wicket gate in the foreground provided access to the boarded crossing leading over the S & W to the GWR station. In 1885, following a request from a Captain Marling, the Severn & Wye agreed to provide a boarded fence, seen to the right of the road vehicle, 'to screen the Company's railway from the road' at a cost of £70. The GWR declined to contribute towards the cost, and it seems likely that, because of this, the Severn & Wye chose to erect only a 70 yard length opposite the site of the original station. In January 1886, following further correspondence with Captain Marling, an additional length of 50 yards was ordered. *L. E. Copeland*

A good view of the sidings from the top of one of the signals shown in the previous photo on 6th September 1947. After passing over the weighbridge, traffic for shipment was sent straight down to the docks where it was sorted for the appropriate coal tip. Both of the lines leading to the harbour were signalled, but in practice the 'down docks' line was used far more than the 'up docks' or loop line. *L. E. Copeland*

The yard was sorted throughout the day with two or three locos often on duty at any one time. This view, taken on 10th April 1948, shows one of the familiar 2021 class 0—6—0PTs at work sorting a few of the endless successions of coal wagons. *L. E. Copeland*

Looking over to the engine shed from the yard box, again on 10th April 1948. The main line to Lydney Town is curving away out of the right of the picture. *L. E. Copeland*

Lydney shed from the north on 30th July 1939 just prior to the outbreak of the Second World War. The three pitched roofs on the left enclosed the repair shop whilst the running shed itself was the main building in the centre of the picture. The separate building on the right was a general stores, which incorporated an office where the crews signed on, and the grounded coach body on the extreme left was provided in 1921 at a cost of £170 17s. 0d. for the use of shedmen and cleaners, the loco crews cabin being considered too small for all three grades of staff. The coal stage was originally constructed of timber and measured some 80 ft x 34 ft, tapering to 13 ft. It was surmounted by a single crane used for hoisting buckets of coal, the operation being carried out by three coalmen on each turn, often assisted by a couple of the six or so cleaners. Engines were loaded from either side of the platform and during the day locos often returned to the shed for a 'couple of tubs', particularly on the 'Lydbrook turn' before continuing on to Berkeley Road. The crane was later condemned, after which locos were coaled directly from wagons, the procedure usually adopted being to shovel supplies simultaneously from wagons either side while locos stood on the centre road of the running shed. Loco coal was obtained from collieries as far afield as Lancaster and Ebbw Vale, Forest coal being unsuitable for locomotive use, and by 1885 the Severn and Wye were sending their own wagons to the collieries for this purpose. Fires were cleaned and dropped on either of the pits alongside the coal platform. The locos on the right are stabled on the siding leading to the tinplate works.

W. A. Camwell

The familiar '2021s' at the shed in 1949. *L & GRP courtesy David & Charles*

LYDNEY ENGINE SHED

The engine shed at Lydney dated from about 1865 when, in March, the Directors resolved that 'an engine house of timber, with work or fitting shop adjoining' should be erected forthwith. It was built on the site then known as Pill House in Church Road and extended in 1868 for two broad gauge engines expected at the time.

It is possible that the shed was rebuilt in 1876 when, following reports in which Messrs. Appleby, Thomlinson and Fisher, three locomotive engineers, described the workshops and fixed machinery as being too limited with regards to both space and power, plans were submitted by G. W.

Keeling for an additional engine shed at an estimated cost of £800. The plans were later modified in order to save £220. In October 1879 additional machinery was purchased to the value of £800 and in December the Midland Locomotive Superintendent at Gloucester, Mr. Clover, was assisting to remodel the 'Company's locomotive establishment'. At the same time a set of shear-legs for lifting engines and a shaping machine were ordered at a cost of about £150. A further £141 5s. 6d. was also spent on additional machinery in 1893.

The shed was enlarged in 1891 to provide an adequate fitting shop and the following year it was decided to build a new stores, foreman's and timekeeper's offices near the

Collett 0—4—2T No. 1404 alongside the coaling stage, and 0—6—0 Dean Goods No. 2350 inside the shed, on 22nd July 1950.

T. J. Edgington

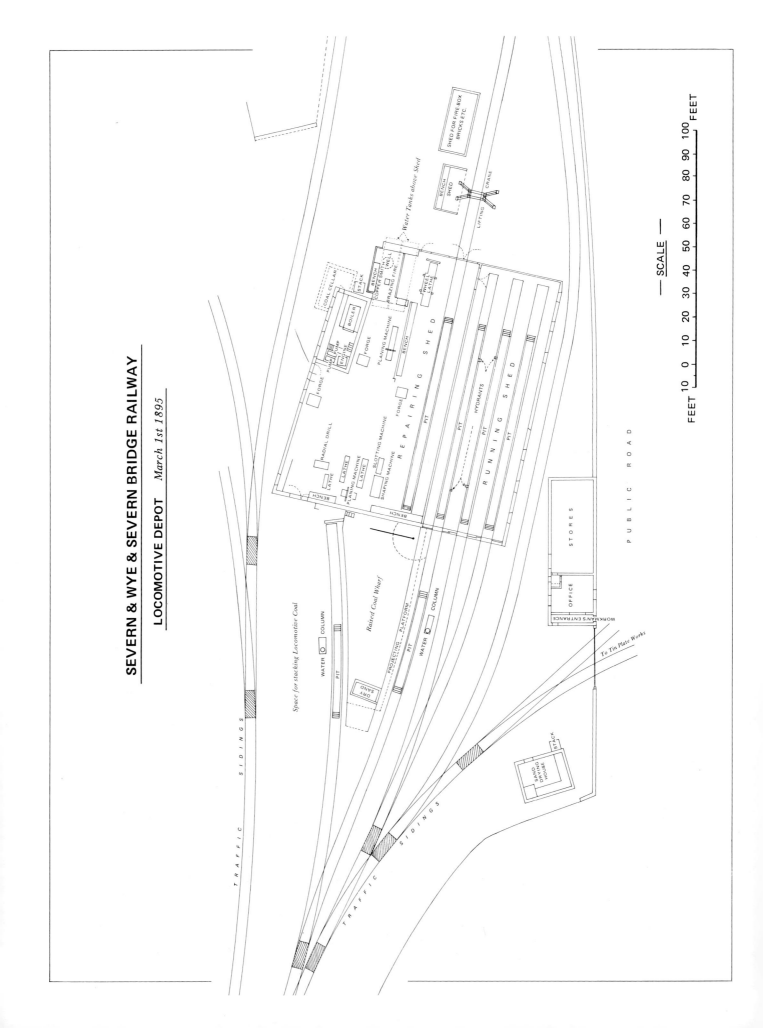

SEVERN & WYE & SEVERN BRIDGE RAILWAY

LOCOMOTIVE DEPOT   *March 1st 1895*

FEET 10 0 10 20 30 40 50 60 70 80 90 100 FEET

— SCALE —

TRAFFIC SIDINGS

Space for stacking Locomotive Coal

WATER COLUMN

Raised Coal Wharf

PROJECTING   PLATFORM

PIT

DRY SAND

WATER COLUMN

TRAFFIC SIDINGS

SAND DRYING HOUSE

STACK

To Tin Plate Works

WORKMAN'S ENTRANCE

OFFICE

STORES

PUBLIC   ROAD

FORGE

PUMP PLUNGE ENGINE

BOILER

FORGE

COAL CELLAR

STACK

BENCH COPPER SMITH

WELL

BRAZING FIRE

WHEEL LATHE

Water Tanks above Shed

BENCH SHED

LIFTING CRANE

SHED FOR FIRE BOX BRICKS ETC.

RADIAL DRILL

LATHE

LATHE

PLANING MACHINE

SLOTTING MACHINE

SHAPING MACHINE

BENCH

FORGE

PLANING MACHINE

BENCH

REPAIRING   SHED

PIT

PIT

PIT

PIT

BENCH

RUNNING SHED

HYDRANTS

0—6—0PT No. 2100 in the shed yard on 10th April 1939. The brick chimney in the foreground is part of the 1910 sandhouse and furnace and the brick hut on the end of the coaling platform had served as a store for dry sand at one time; latterly it was used to store equipment for the coalmen. *V. R. Webster*

entrance gates. The existing stores, 'very cramped and insufficient', was instead converted into a boiler and pump house which would otherwise have been built. The new stores and office building was in use by April 1894.

By 1897 the shed was officially recorded as having stone walls with wooden gable ends and a slate roof, its inside dimensions being 114 ft 6 ins long, 36 ft 6 ins wide, with a height to the top of the roof ridge and wall plate of 28 ft and 15 ft 4 ins respectively. It spanned three lines which terminated inside, each 111 ft long with 84 ft long pits.

Repairs were carried out in the adjoining repair or erecting shop which was served by a single track that entered from the rear. It was again built of stone with a gable style slate roof and wooden ends, with inside dimensions of 114 ft long by 23 ft wide and heights to the ridge and wall plate of 26 ft 9 ins and 14 ft 6 ins. The facilities, which included forges, lathes (including a wheel lathe supplied in 1885 at a cost of £310), planing, shaping and drilling machines etc., were used to the full, jobs carried out during the line's independence including gauge alterations, cylinder boring, reboilering etc. However, even during the last years of the company, engines were sometimes sent to Avonside for overhaul. When the Joint Committee took over, much of the equipment in the repair shop was disposed of between the two companies, but the depot nevertheless continued retubing and boiler work, the workshops being staffed by a boilersmith and mate, a chargeman fitter, two fitters and two mates.

By 1903 the shed had fallen into disrepair, Johnson and Churchward, Locomotive Superintendents of the MR and GWR respectively, describing it as being in 'very bad condition'. Their report that April stated that 1600 slates were required for the roof as well as new battens. The roof lights needed repair and reglazing and the stack pipes and sand furnace also needed repairing. There were no smoke troughs at this time so these were also recommended, together with a chimney in the fitting shop and a drain

from the office. The estimated cost of the work was £80. What work was done at this time is not clear, particularly as further repairs and improvements estimated at some £625 were carried out by January 1910. The sandhouse and furnace were rebuilt by April 1910 at an estimated cost of £20, the original being replaced by a standard GWR corrugated iron structure. Smoke troughs were also provided (or renewed?) in 1924 for £180.

In the 1920s some 14 locos were shedded at Lydney to cover the 13 S & W turns. They were mainly '2021' class 0—6—0PTs but in addition the allocation also included

Driver Vic Rees at the signing-on point in the office. The major part of this building housed the Loco Dept. stores, the storekeeper starting at 5.45 a.m. each day to issue each of the crews with their brass check. Oil and cotton waste were also issued each day but loco tools were kept in the enginemen's mess. The stores were closed at 5.30 p.m. after which only the shed foreman had a set of keys. *A. K. Pope*

A 1950s view of the shed showing a much clearer view of the stores and sandhouse. Sand arrived in trucks and was usually unloaded by a couple of cleaners, the shedman keeping the fire going all the time. Oil was delivered in barrels and in 1914 the Joint Committee agreed to improve the arrangements for handling these barrels at an estimated cost of £8 10s., but the nature of these improvements is not known.

R. Dagley Morris

A much later view of the shed during the final years, showing the new corrugated asbestos roof. The sliding doors featured on previous views were frequently repaired after numerous mishaps over the years — usually resulting from younger members of the Loco Dept. moving locos with insufficient steam pressure to operate the steam brake!

A. K. Pope

0—4—2T No. 1404 and 0—6—0PT No. 2131 outside the shed, probably during the late 1940s. The 0—4—2Ts were kept at Lydney for the Berkeley auto services, not being at all suitable for the demands of the heavy mineral traffic.
Lens of Sutton

three tender locos for the double home turns to Stoke Gifford and Weston Super Mare and Taunton. 0—6—0 Dean Goods were usually provided for these turns but from about 1948 they were succeeded by '53XX' class Moguls. The small shed became somewhat congested when the engines returned at night, a number of them being stored outside on any of the seven lines of 344 ft, 138 ft, 134 ft, 122 ft, 127 ft, 33 ft and 33 ft length, those either side of the coal platform incorporating pits of 46 ft and 41 ft. The lengths specified include the lines at the side and rear of the shed which were mainly used for storage including locos awaiting attention.

A line up of '2021s' behind the shed was once a familiar sight alongside Church Road. This particular view shows Nos. 2131, 2029, 2155 and another unidentified half cab on 10th April 1939.
V. R. Webster

The rear of the shed during the final years, again showing the new roof.   *A. K. Pope*

A closer view showing the entrance to the repair shops. The line, which extended 103 ft inside, incorporating an 82 ft 6 ins pit, was formerly straddled by shear-legs with a shed and crane as shown on the 1895 site plan. The shear-legs survived the initial clearing out of machinery by the Joint Committee, but were apparently never used after 1895, being condemned as obsolete in March 1913 by the Joint CMEs, Churchward and Fowler.

The twin water tanks (believed to have been two old boilers purchased from the Gloucester & Berkeley Canal Co. in 1881) supplied the two water columns outside the shed, 4 hydrants and the water crane at the end of the 'down' platform. Water was pumped from a well beneath the brick base using a small steam engine powered from a stationary boiler. This was formerly located in part of the repair shop, to the right of the picture, coal supplies being kept in a cellar beneath. The pumps were tended by a full time pumpman who for many years was Harry Imm; however, at night when they were often still required, they were manned by the night foreman. The pumps remained in the old room but the boiler was later replaced by the one illustrated which also supplied hot water for washouts. The supply came from Messrs. Thomas' canal, but by 1885 it was reported as 'bad for engines' and pipes were laid to Plummers Brook. By 1896 the supply came partly from a reservoir gravity fed from 'a stream' (presumably Plummers Brook), but in 1905 it was again reported as coming partly from the canal. This was still of unsatisfactory quality because of contamination from the tinworks and an increased supply was therefore obtained from the River Lyd at a cost of some £60. Whilst details are not clear, this was probably when the corrugated iron 'pump house' referred to on page 44 was installed. It seems that this building housed the inlet pipe and the all essential filters. By 1911 the Severn & Wye were making an annual payment to the Great Western for the supply of water to the engine shed, but to confuse matters it is recorded that in 1921 the GW were proposing to obtain their water supply from the S & W pumping station in order to be able to close their own pumping plant, but the outcome is unconfirmed.

W. Potter

Two views inside the repair shed during the final years.

R. Marrows

The sidings serving Lydney tinplate works stemmed from the edge of the shed yard to the right of the picture. This view, taken from Lydney Engine Shed signal box on 10th April 1948, just shows the location of the canal behind the low embankment to the right.   *L. E. Copeland*

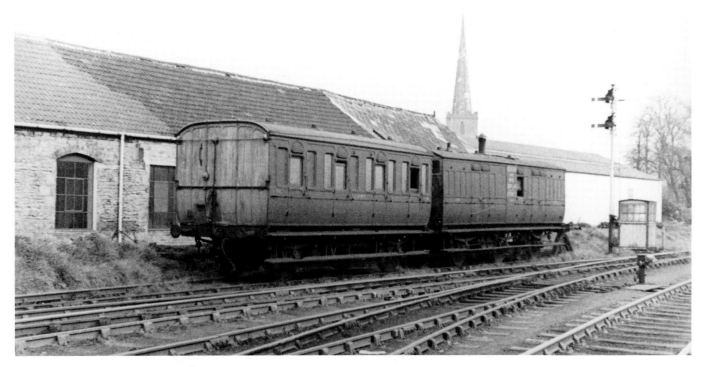

The Lydney breakdown train, again on 10th April 1948. A breakdown van was first purchased by the Joint Committee from the GW for £80 in 1913. Space was always at a premium at the shed so it is hardly surprising that the 'headshunt' was then extended early in 1914 to provide a readily accessible home for it. The extension cost some £35 but a further £9 was also subsequently spent on lighting the vehicle with a standard Great Western acetylene lamp. Although of Great Western origin, neither of the vehicles shown were originally intended for use in breakdown trains. The nearer, No. 74, is an ex- 4-wheeled 4-compartment 1st carriage of Holden's 'Metro' suburban stock, built in 1898 to Diagram R3 as part of Lot 877. In 1907 it became composite No. 6116, in 1936 a workmen's third No. 707 and in 1940 a breakdown van as shown. It was condemned in July 1954. The van is No. 575, a former 6-wheeled arc-roofed passenger brake van built in 1884 to Diagram V13, and still retaining its original clasp brake gear. It was converted for use as a breakdown van in 1926 and at the time of this photograph was lettered 'Severn & Wye Joint Line, Lydney, GWR'.

With the constant movement of huge numbers of wagons throughout the day and much of the night, derailments were inevitable and the breakdown train was in frequent use all over the system, but particularly in the numerous colliery owned sidings where wagons often jumped the track. The train was generally taken to even minor derailments so that all necessary equipment was on hand. It was usually hauled by a spare engine and manned by the shed foreman and one or two shedmen or cleaners. The van contained various jacks, packing blocks, ropes and chains, crowbars, etc. The Engine Shed ground frame or 'stage' shown alongside the signal, was a standard MR design.   *L. E. Copeland*

Two views of 'Lydney Engine Shed' signal box in 1964 and 1933 respectively. This was a standard Midland Railway structure supplied at a cost of £639 by that company during resignalling work in 1918. At this time the GWR were concerned about the unsatisfactory sighting of trains at Lydney Junction station and pressed for track circuiting to be included in the resignalling scheme. However, the Midland, who were responsible for signalling this section of the line, would not agree, and the work was deferred. Nevertheless, further improvements were made including, in 1920, provision for operating the points leading to the engine shed from the box. The signalman here called the time to loco crews when booking them off shed. He also logged their return and the S & W inspector made random checks to compare the signalman's record against the engineman's log. The S & W were paying for engine time and this unofficial local arrangement was intended to make both records agree and save a lot of questions!

R. Marrows and L. E. Copeland

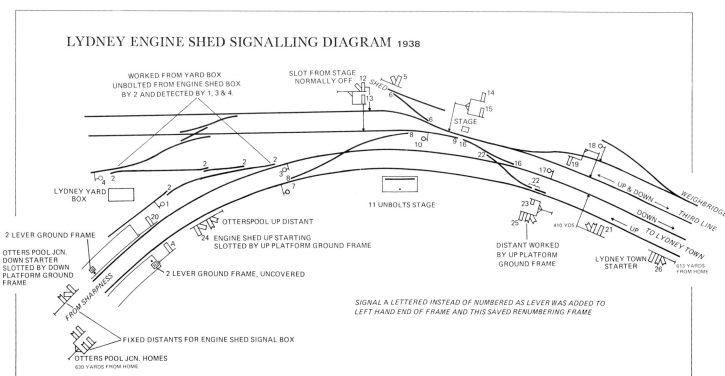

LYDNEY ENGINE SHED GROUND FRAME 1938

unbolted by lever 11 in Engine Shed box. This allowed locomotive crews to come off shed when Engine Shed box was unmanned.

STANDS NORMALLY OFF

slots points also worked from Engine Shed box.

STAGE

DOWN →

← UP

FROM LYDNEY JUNCTION

TO LYDNEY TOWN

LYDNEY ENGINE SHED SIGNAL BOX

LYDNEY ENGINE SHED SIGNALLING DIAGRAM 1938

WORKED FROM YARD BOX
UNBOLTED FROM ENGINE SHED BOX
BY 2 AND DETECTED BY 1, 3 & 4.

SLOT FROM STAGE
NORMALLY OFF

SHED

STAGE

LYDNEY YARD BOX

11 UNBOLTS STAGE

WEIGHBRIDGE

UP & DOWN

DOWN

UP TO LYDNEY TOWN

THIRD LINE

DISTANT WORKED
BY UP PLATFORM
GROUND FRAME

LYDNEY TOWN STARTER

613 YARDS FROM HOME

410 YDS

2 LEVER GROUND FRAME

OTTERS POOL JCN.
DOWN STARTER
SLOTTED BY DOWN
PLATFORM GROUND
FRAME

OTTERSPOOL UP DISTANT

ENGINE SHED UP STARTING
SLOTTED BY UP PLATFORM GROUND FRAME

2 LEVER GROUND FRAME, UNCOVERED

FROM SHARPNESS

FIXED DISTANTS FOR ENGINE SHED SIGNAL BOX

OTTERS POOL JCN. HOMES
630 YARDS FROM HOME

*SIGNAL A LETTERED INSTEAD OF NUMBERED AS LEVER WAS ADDED TO
LEFT HAND END OF FRAME AND THIS SAVED RENUMBERING FRAME*

This 1929 view, dominated by St. Mary's church, not only shows the relationship of the tinplate works to the engine shed (bottom left) but also features a pannier tank crossing Church Road in the course of servicing the private siding. The long low buildings in the centre of the picture had previously been a colour works, but by this time were occupied by the West of England Wagon Co.

Aerofilms

A view taken from St. Mary's church tower looking along Church Road c.1900. The tinplate works can be seen on the right hand side of the road whilst the engine shed is on the left.

Collection N. Parkhouse

LYDNEY TINPLATE WORKS

The Lydney tinplate works at Lower Forge was served by two sidings which, stemming from the edge of the loco yard, led across Church Road and into the premises. The two sidings ran either side of the works and were known as the North and South Sidings respectively, the former being the oldest, dating from at least 1877. The works originally formed part of a much larger complex which also included the Middle and Upper Forges and later the New Mills, all further up the valley of the River Lyd between Lydney Town and Tufts Junction.

Tinplate is sheet steel, originally sheet iron, coated with a thin protective layer of tin. Raw iron was brought into the works in the form of ingots which were then heated and rolled into flat sheets through the rolling mills. The sheets were then cut into plates using power shears, cleansed in acid, annealed, tinned and packed into boxes ready for shipping. The manufacturing process was a hazardous occupation, many accidents occurring with either the acid baths or the shears.

It is possible that tinplate was being produced at Lydney in 1781, at which time the complex of ironworks was being leased from the Bathurst family, owners of the Lydney Park Estate, by David Tanner. Tinplate was certainly being produced in 1798, when the lessees of the works were Thomas and John Pidcock and George Homfray who had acquired the lease in 1790. To facilitate the movement of materials between the Upper, Middle and Lower Forges they had, by 1800, constructed a canal between Middle Forge and the River Severn at Lydney Pill. In 1810 when the Severn & Wye were building their tramroad, they were

authorized to 'cross the private canal . . . twice by a draw-bridge'.

In November 1813 the Pidcocks assigned their interest back to the landowner, the Rt. Hon. Charles Bathurst who, in 1814, leased the works to John James who also had an interest in the Redbrook Tinplate Works on the River Wye. James, in 1814, connected the Upper, Middle and Lower Forges to the Severn & Wye tramroad and, in 1824, added to the complex of ironworks by building the New Mills between the Upper and Middle Forges. The lease was surrendered in 1847 and Bathurst re-let the works to the Allaways:- William, Stephen, William the younger and Thomas, all ironmasters and tinplate manufacturers, and James Allaway, a banker, the family already owning the Lydbrook Tinplate Works.

In 1875 Richard Thomas and Sons acquired the lease and all other interests of the Allaways and very soon ran into a series of disputes with the Severn & Wye. Although a standard gauge siding had been laid near the New Mills in 1873, Thomas was still using the tramroad to convey his materials in 1879. The Severn & Wye had been wanting to remove this last remaining section of the main line tramroad since 1875 but Charles Bathurst, as landowner, objected to its removal until his lease on various collieries ran out in 1879. Accordingly, that year the Severn & Wye notified Thomas of their intention to remove the line, Thomas objected and gained a six months stay of execution. He then suggested that he might lay his own private tramroad on the course of Pidcock's Canal, which would include the construction of a subway under the railway near Lydney church. The Severn & Wye agreed to this as long as Thomas did not convey coal, coke or pig-iron upon the line without

A general view of the works, with the level crossing off to the right (out of the picture), featuring stacks of boxes into which the finished tinplate was packed for dispatch. The works chimneys were a notable landmark. For many years the tallest had been 164 ft high. It was built in 1882 'to alleviate a smoke problem', but was surpassed in 1913 by another, 174 ft high.
Collection E. Gwynne

paying compensation to the company, but as these three commodities would have been the bulk of Thomas's traffic, nothing came of the scheme. The six months stay of execution appears to have been rather flexible as in May 1882 the Board called Thomas's attention to the tramroad and stated that it would be removed on 1st December. Part of the line was indeed removed, but again Thomas got a three months extension of time until March, when the tramway was removed 'at places dangerous to the railway'. The remainder was left for a further three months after which time it too was removed.

Meanwhile in January 1883 Thomas had asked the Severn & Wye to provide permanent way materials to lay new sidings at Lower Forge and to lower the rates on traffic between that place and Middle Forge 'as the Severn & Wye had not been asked to build the subway near the Church'. The Severn & Wye eventually offered the permanent way materials but the tinplate company refused the offer, as they were in financial difficulties. The works had closed earlier in the year and the company went into liquidation in July. The Severn & Wye offer was withdrawn when it too went into liquidation later in the year.

R. Thomas & Co. were solvent again by February 1884 but it was not until January 1885 that the dispute was finally resolved, with Thomas having to settle for a reduction in the rates only. Within eight months a further dispute arose when the Severn & Wye refused to provide wagons for the tinplate traffic owing to a shortage of rolling stock and the excessive time that loaded wagons were retained at the works.

An interesting aside is that while the dispute over the tramroad was proceeding, Richard Thomas was elected to the Board of Directors of the Severn & Wye, only to resign when his company went into liquidation. Richard Thomas was succeeded at the works by his son, R. Beaumont Thomas, in 1888 and the company entered a new period of prosperity. By 1891 only the Lower Forge was operating, all production being concentrated there whilst the other works were demolished.

Finished tinplate from the works was carried in boxes down Thomas's own tramway to a warehouse situated alongside Pidcock's Canal, then on to a 'free-wharf' at the head of the Severn & Wye Canal. From here the boxes of tinplate were loaded onto a small steamboat, called the *Black Dwarf*, for passage to Avonmouth. The tinplate company enjoyed free use of the wharf and waterways as the construction of the Severn & Wye had disrupted their predecessors' freedom of access to the River Severn, via the original natural Lydney Pill.

During the Second World War the works were requisitioned by the Admiralty and reopened under the management of Richard Thomas & Baldwin. In 1946 five of the eleven rolling mills were shut down and in May 1947 the works were taken over by the Steel Company of Wales. The remaining rolling mills were shut down in 1957 and the sidings removed in 1960.

A closer view of some of the works buildings.

Collection N. Parkhouse

Traffic to and from the works was hauled by the Joint Committee's engines, but no agreement could be reached over relieving the Committee from liability in the case of any accident or mishap that might have occurred while traffic was being shunted over the level crossing. Consequently, at the end of October 1899, the Committee gave Thomas & Co. three months notice to terminate the existing agreement, and stated that if the firm wanted the Committee's engines to pass onto their works they would have to take responsibility. The immediate outcome is not recorded, but the matter was evidently settled as the Committee's engines continued to service the works.

The following instructions for operating the sidings appeared in subsequent working appendices:

Shunting at Tinplate works siding Lydney Junction
The gates across the line leading to the tinplate works at Lydney Junction must be kept closed and locked. When it is necessary to put into or take traffic out of the works the shunter must go in advance of the train, open the gates, secure them, and satisfy himself that the public highway is clear of vehicles, foot passengers and other traffic, and co-operate with the tinplate company's gate-keeper in protecting the public.

In 1920 the tinplate company provided an additional siding within the works and asked the Joint Committee to deliver traffic and perform shunting duties similar to those carried out at the existing sidings.

Keen to establish a basis for raising the charges, the Committee arranged a survey of the time spent shunting the enlarged layout. However, it quickly transpired that the improvements meant that time spent shunting the works had actually decreased by about 10 minutes per day to an average of 2 hours, whilst the number of wagons dealt with remained the same at 32 per day. Not surprisingly, it was decided that there was no case for asking Thomas & Co. to pay increased charges!

The tinworks steam crane operating amongst the stack of cut steel sheets prior to their passing through the plating process. In 1917 the Joint Committee refused permission for the crane to enter the loco yard for shunting purposes.

Collection E. Gwynne

Glantawe, an Andrew Barclay locomotive, standing just inside the works yard near the Church Road level crossing.   *Rev. D. A. Tipper*

One of the Steel Company of Wales' locomotives, a Hudswell Clarke named *Peter Pan*, sorting wagons amidst the steel sheet within the works.

L. E. Copeland

Looking into the tinworks yard from Church Road at the point where the sidings entered the works premises. The Steel Company of Wales' flag is shown at half mast to mark the closure of the works. *Courtesy J. Powell*

Certainly until the Second World War the railway company's engines carried out all the necessary shunting. An old Lydney driver recalls that during the 1930s the works were shunted every morning for about an hour or so, much of which was spent crossing the public road. In subsequent years, possibly from the Steel Company of Wales' takeover, at least two of their own locomotives were employed within the works. In August 1948 a Railway Executive memorandum stated that engine stop boards had been fixed inside the works yard at 40 yards on the works side of the crossing on the North Sidings and 440 yards past the crossing on the South Sidings.

It was also stated that when the tinplate company's engine required to pass between their two fans of internal sidings and the Railway Executive's Locomotive Yard connections, the firm's shunter should first obtain permission from the man in charge at the Locomotive Department, who would advise the signalman at the Engine Shed signal box of the requirements. The shunt was not to be allowed to proceed beyond the outlet signal from the locomotive sidings.

The majority of the tinplate works buildings have now been demolished, but the remainder are still in use for general industrial purposes.

The gated entrance on the opposite side of Church Road leading into the engine shed yard. The doorway in the building led into the lobby where locomotive crews booked on duty, as seen on page 55.   *R. Marrows*

Looking north from the Engine Shed box with the West of England Wagon works siding being serviced on 19th April 1948. The running crossover in the foreground was officially known as 'Tinworks Junction'. *L. E. Copeland*

The cast iron lattice footbridge just beyond Churchfield occupation level crossing was first opened to the public on 26th September 1892. It was provided to combat the 'serious trespass that has grown up by the workmen and others walking over the company's railway between the engine shed and tinplate sidings and the church, the excuse being that the coal trains standing on the company's railway opposite the church prevented them from using the public footpath through the churchyard and crossing the railway at that point'. The structure was ordered from Messrs. G. Smith & Co. of Glasgow who were to deliver and erect it for £247, the S & W

preparing the foundations. The cost was in fact exceeded by £20 when it was found necessary to increase the span and lengthen the stairs.

The bridge was a great source of attraction to the local children who were apparently in the habit of sliding down the handrails, and in 1901 the Lydney local authorities pointed out the potential danger of the culprits falling off and becoming impaled on the iron railings beneath. The Committee agreed and scotched the practice for a cost of 30 shillings simply by fixing iron nuts at intervals along the handrails. *R. Marrows*

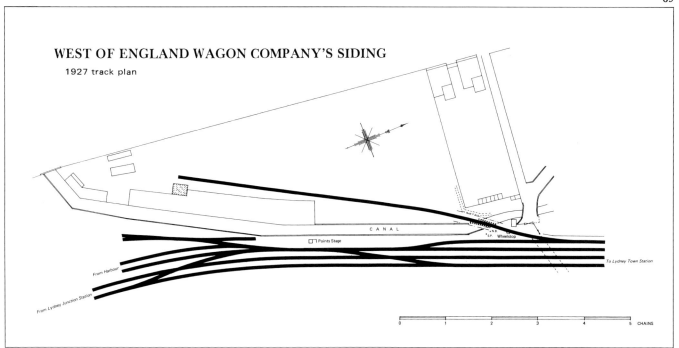

WEST OF ENGLAND WAGON COMPANY'S SIDING

1927 track plan

CANAL

☐ Points Stage

Wheelstop

From Harbour

From Lydney Junction Station

To Lydney Town Station

0 1 2 3 4 5 CHAINS

LYDNEY COLOUR WORKS

The siding to the north of Lydney engine shed, which latterly became the West of England Wagon Company's private siding, originally served a colour works. Colour is a ferric oxide which occurs in an oily mass alongside the iron-ores of the crease limestone. It is red by nature and was used by paint manufacturers in the production of oil paints. Colour was generally found underlying the iron-ores but it was never found in large quantities and therefore commanded a reasonably high price. Iron miners often hoped to find a good deposit, or 'churn', of colour in preference to the iron-ore itself, but due to its scarcity they were often disappointed.

There were several colour works within the Forest, mainly on the western side, although the best colour was found in the Cinderford area at the Buckshaft Mine. This was known as 'Crawshay red' and, world renowned, acted as the measure by which all other red oxides were graded.

Colour works are not to be confused with ochre works which also existed in the Forest. Ochre is a hydrated oxide of iron, usually yellow or brown in nature.

The buildings housing the colour works were certainly in existence by 1877 when they are shown on Severn & Wye plans as a sawmills served by a siding. In 1886 the buildings were taken over by William Jones and Company to house their firm's colour works. Previously they had leased Severn & Wye land alongside the canal in Lydney Basin. The firm applied for a junction to a siding into their works, which suggests that either the original saw-mills siding had been removed at some stage, or that the points only had been taken out or broken.

Subsequently rates of 8d for owners wagons and 9d for Severn & Wye wagons were agreed on the understanding that competitive traffic was 'to pass over the Severn Bridge route'.

During the next decade the firm underwent several changes of name. By 1889 they were trading as Wellington, Jones and White & Company and in 1897 as Wellington, Jones & Company, Colour Manufacturers, Church Road, Lydney, and were sending 'red ochre powder' in barrels

from the works. At some point between 1910 and 1914 the concern passed into the hands of Hickling & Evans. The exact closure date of the colour works is unknown, but in 1925 the buildings housed the West of England Wagon Company.

This company, owned by William Wentworth of Gloucester and Percy Moore of Aylburton near Lydney, started in 1920 and originally occupied a hut in the Junction Yard close to the footbridge. In 1925 they moved to the old colour works premises and took out a siding agreement with the LMS and GW in August 1927 for the existing siding for a yearly rental of £3. Traffic for the siding was charged at 6d per wagon in each direction plus the normal rates of carriage applicable at the time, charged from Lydney station. Although the siding agreement was terminated in 1959 and the siding removed in November 1960, the wagon company continued trading until they went into liquidation in 1962. The buildings still stand today and now house an engineering works.

The entrance to the West of England Wagon Co.'s private siding which bridged the canal.
L. E. Copeland

An unidentified '2021' class pannier tank running towards Lydney Junction during Easter 1935 with what is almost certainly an excursion train from Lydney Town.

Collection P. Karau

Opposite: The view south from the footbridge on 17th August 1956. The third line from the left extended from Lydney Town where all mineral trains from the Forest were routed over it for checking or in order to pass over the wagon weighbridge situated just beyond the footbridge on the loop line. It is not difficult to appreciate the resulting congestion. The original weighing machine was situated further south by the entrance to what was once the sawmill siding. It was first provided in 1869 by Messrs. Pooley & Son and used for weighing broad gauge vehicles. The cottage for the machine keeper was also provided at the time for some £200. In 1874-5, prior to the commencement of passenger services, the line between Lydney Junction and Lydney Town was doubled, leaving the original line solely for mineral traffic. In 1887 another line was added to give separate 'up' and 'down' running lines and c.1889 the weighing machine was resited on a new loop line (laid on the site of the former tramroad) on the right of the photo alongside the third line. The bulk of traffic was weighed at the originating collieries but many wagons were weighed here and every one was checked at Lydney, the guard picking up traffic and consignment notes for each wagon bound for the docks. The notes were subsequently checked by the Lydney weighbridge clerk with the records of the number-taker on duty between 9.00 a.m. and 7.30 p.m., and then taken to the mineral office where they were sorted and entered each day in the Lydney Docks book. This all important procedure enabled a summary to be made at the end of each month for entering onto traders' accounts. All wagons going to the docks were recorded in the wagon book at Lydney Junction and checked with the invoices. The invoices abstracted at the docks were then checked with a similar document prepared in the mineral office.

Through traffic leaving the Severn & Wye at Bilson and Lydbrook Junctions was recorded daily by Drybrook Road and Lydbrook respectively, their returns being sent to the mineral office each morning where each wagon was checked and compared with the invoice. However, 'owing to want of staff' no such check was made in respect of traffic leaving the S & W at Lydney so in 1906, when the matter was brought to the Committee's attention, it was resolved to employ a number-taker there.

The mineral line was used by 'down' trains if the 'down' running line was blocked, but by 1906 it was used in the mornings solely for shunting and weighbridge purposes from the south, and after 11 a.m. only for 'up' trains.

Below: the machine keeper's cottage.

L. E. Copeland and Rev. D. A. Tipper

A 1929 aerial view, looking up the valley of the Lyd towards Norchard Colliery and the power station, which are seen at the top right. Pidcock's Canal is also prominent in the foreground, the railway running almost parallel here. The Severn & Wye offices in Lydney are in the exact centre of the photograph, close to Lydney Town station. The foundry siding is *in situ*, although by this time serving Arnold Perrett & Co.'s brewery stores.

Aerofilms

A postcard view of Lydney Town station, probably c.1905.

Lens of Sutton

LYDNEY TOWN

This was the local station for the inhabitants of Lydney and was conveniently situated close to the town centre. Goods traffic for the town was also dealt with here but the station owed its operational importance to the fact that the double track from Lydney Junction ended here. The following section to Tufts Junction was controlled by a single line tablet system installed in 1887 to replace the staff and ticket system formerly used. The third or mineral line running south to the weighbridge also commenced from the foot of the platforms.

Facilities were originally much simpler, one of the small 20 ft wooden buildings being provided by Eassie & Co. as featured above. However, whilst these original buildings were adequate for the more isolated stations, it is not surprising that the inhabitants of Lydney should send a memorial to the Committee in June 1896 requesting better accommodation. The Committee evidently accepted the shortcomings of their facilities and the provision of a new building was approved at an estimated cost of £620.

The new building, completed the following year, was a vast improvement, being constructed of red brick to a contemporary standard GWR design and situated on the 'down' platform opposite the original. The level crossing and signalling here were also undergoing improvements at this time, a new signal box controlling the gates of this busy crossing. The new arrangements were inspected by the Board of Trade on 13th October 1897. The inspecting officer reported:

> 'this station has two platforms 2′ 6″ and new waiting accommodation including conveniences for both sexes has been provided on the main platforms. The lines at the north end of the station

have been slewed, the junction between the double and single lines has been slightly altered in position, the sidings rearranged and the whole place resignalled and interlocked. A new signal box has been built containing 26 levers in use, 5 spare levers, 1 gate wheel and an additional lever for controlling the wicket gate.

The estimated cost of the improvements to the level crossing and the entrance to the goods yard was £695. However, the total outlay exceeded the estimate by £168 14s. 0d., mainly due to extra unclimbable iron fencing in lieu of space and pale, the erection of a porch, pitching the approach road, alterations to platforms 'consequent on slewing lines to give greater space at the entrance of the approach road', and the 'exceptional method' of fixing the level crossing gates.

The former stone-built signal box on the platform was converted into offices for the station master and parcels at a cost of £65. and the hut previously used by the gatekeeper was refixed at Lydney Junction for the accommodation of number-takers. The superstructure of the old box is believed to have been incorporated in the Serridge Junction cabin. It was also decided that the building, which until this time had been occupied by the parcels agent, should be utilized for lamp and mess rooms 'so as to enable the practice which now prevails of staff using the signal box for these purposes to be discontinued'.

The Committee had felt that the existing cartage agent was unsatisfactory and in 1897 resolved that the service should be performed with their own team. The appointed agent had used a horse lorry belonging to the Joint Companies, so it was decided to purchase a horse and employ a carman for the purpose and, 'at a small outlay' to fit up a stables on joint property.

The Committee had been prompt in their response with the new building, but not so co-operative over local com-

plaints of the inconvenience caused by the level crossing dividing Hill Street. The company had been summonsed in 1874 following a complaint of obstruction at Lydney Town crossing, but after G. B. and G. W. Keeling had explained the matter to the Justices, it was decided to leave the matter in abeyance. In April 1900 the local authorities requested a footbridge, but the Committee contended that the only satisfactory arrangement would be the provision of a public road over- or under-bridge by the local authorities. The Lydney authorities subsequently called in the Board of Trade over the matter and in July 1901 Colonel Yorke looked at the crossing and recommended a footbridge. However, the Committee held their ground, claiming that the road and wicket gates were all interlocked and the local people only suffered the inconvenience of short delays.

In October the Lydney Parish Council complained again to the Board of Trade about the shunting over the crossing and the Government Inspector requested a return showing the period impassable. The following January it transpired that delays at the crossing during a week were as follows: 64 vehicles detained 155 minutes — average 2 mins 2 secs each. 153 passengers detained 135 minutes — average 53 secs each.

In April the Board of Trade pointed out the Committee's obligation under the Railway Clauses Act of 1863 to carry any public road over the railway by a bridge if required by the Department to do so. The minutes record no further mention of the Committee's prior recommendation of a road overbridge, but a footbridge was (perhaps almost eagerly) authorized at an estimated cost of £567. The contractors were Messrs. Cross & Cross who completed the long awaited structure in January 1904.

In 1928 the station was staffed by a station master, class 3; two general clerks, class 5; two porters, class 2; two checkers, one of whom worked part time at Lydney dock; and two signalmen, class 4. Three mineral clerks also came under the Lydney Town administration as did three signalmen, class 4, for Engine Shed 'box; two class 5 for Otters

Pool 'box; two class 6 for the Yard 'box and three relief signalmen.

THE FOUNDRY SIDING

The foundry situated behind the 'up' platform predated the station. In 1856 Messrs. Talbot and Grice were trading from here as the Severn & Wye Foundry Company, the land being conveyed to the Severn & Wye Railway Co. from the Bathursts from whom it had previously been rented.

By November 1872 the lessee was T. G. Pearce, who went into liquidation in May 1879. It was then leased to a Mr. Griffiths until December 1881, and in 1888 the Severn & Wye's cartage agent Mr. Mallard applied to use one of the buildings in the foundry yard as a temporary stable. In 1892 the buildings underwent a change of use when Arnold Perrett and Company of Wickwar leased the property as a store for beer, wine and aerated waters. The 1911 S & W Appendix contains instructions to be observed in shunting vehicles into and out of the siding leading to Messrs. Arnold Perrett & Company's stores.

> Before any vehicle is moved into or out of the siding the person in charge of the shunting operations must satisfy himself that no one is standing in or about the siding in precisely the same way as he would be required to do by Rule 112a if the siding were used for loading and unloading purposes.

Old Lydney drivers can remember working into this siding with vans and recall that there was always a barrel of beer tapped in the yard. Needless to say, servicing the siding was always popular with the crews!

The siding was removed in 1933 but the buildings survived until 1969.

From July 1920 Perrett's also leased the Railway Hotel at Lydney Docks from the Severn & Wye. In 1912, the Anglo-Bavarian Brewery Co. Ltd. had a lease from the Severn & Wye of unspecified land at Lydney Town station with permission to erect a store house thereon, but nothing else has so far been discovered about this.

Opposite: The southern approach to Lydney Town on 26th March 1948. The goods yard on the left led off the commencement of the third or mineral line to Lydney Junction and was provided with a standard 'Gloucester' goods shed in 1880. The left of two short spur sidings on the left (out of the picture) served a cattle dock. This was provided in 1893 on land then recently acquired from Mr. Bathurst who objected to the pens on the grounds that 'they may become a nuisance'. Certainly after the Great War this was hardly used. There was also a dock or 'carriage shoot' presumably on the other spur for which a winch was provided in 1906. It is not clear what prompted its provision but it was intended to stop vehicles running down the slope and endangering traffic. In 1913, following reports that the arrangements for dealing with horse and carriage traffic were 'very inconvenient', improvements were carried out to the dock which necessitated the widening of the approach at the end nearest the entrance from Hill Street.

The yard also contained a well and in 1898 horse pumping gear was installed in order to provide an additional supply of water to the station buildings. The installation was proposed as a temporary measure in view of the probability of the Local Authorities establishing a new water supply, and the horse gear was declared obsolete and removed in 1913.

The gate just visible on the right had formerly closed across Arnold Perrett's private siding. An unusual arrangement here was that in 1893 the S & W ordered a small open corrugated iron carriage shed which was erected over the siding just inside the gate. It was 100 ft long and provided by Messrs. Lysaght & Co. (Bristol) for £61. It was used to stable the three carriages of the last train from the Forest. It would appear that in placing the carriages on this siding, accidents had occurred as the general appendix carried the following instruction:

Shunting at Lydney Town leading to Foundry Yard

Accidents have occurred to the doors at the end of this siding through putting away carriages into the shelter at Lydney Town when a wagon is standing on the siding.

Guards putting away coaches into the siding must be very careful to see that the siding is clear before backing the train. When, however, a wagon is standing in the siding the guard in

charge must, before signalling the train to back, see that the brakes on the standing truck are firmly pinned down, and must remain by the wagon until the coaches are brought to a stand-still.

In all cases Drivers must use great caution when pushing back. When the siding contains more than one wagon the coaches must be put into the Lydney Goods Yard, and the same care must be taken by the guard in charge not to damage the Goods Yard doors . . . . .

By 1907 the carriage shed was apparently no longer required and the need for repairs prompted the decision in September that year to remove it.

L. E. Copeland

This mystery building was latterly used as a stores for the Signal and Telegraph Department, but an 1881 track plan clearly shows a loop siding running right through it. The wooden-end wall enclosing the former rail entrance appears to have been of Midland origin and presumably a post-1906 addition. The water tower may have been added in 1897 when the Committee decided to establish a stables here, as old staff seem to remember it in use as such. It is also believed to have incorporated a blacksmith's shop. *Rev. D. A. Tipper*

Taken from the entrance to the goods yard, this 1966 view shows the Gloucester Wagon Co. goods shed and, in the background, the northern end of the 'mystery building', again featuring distinctive Midland windows.

R. Marrows

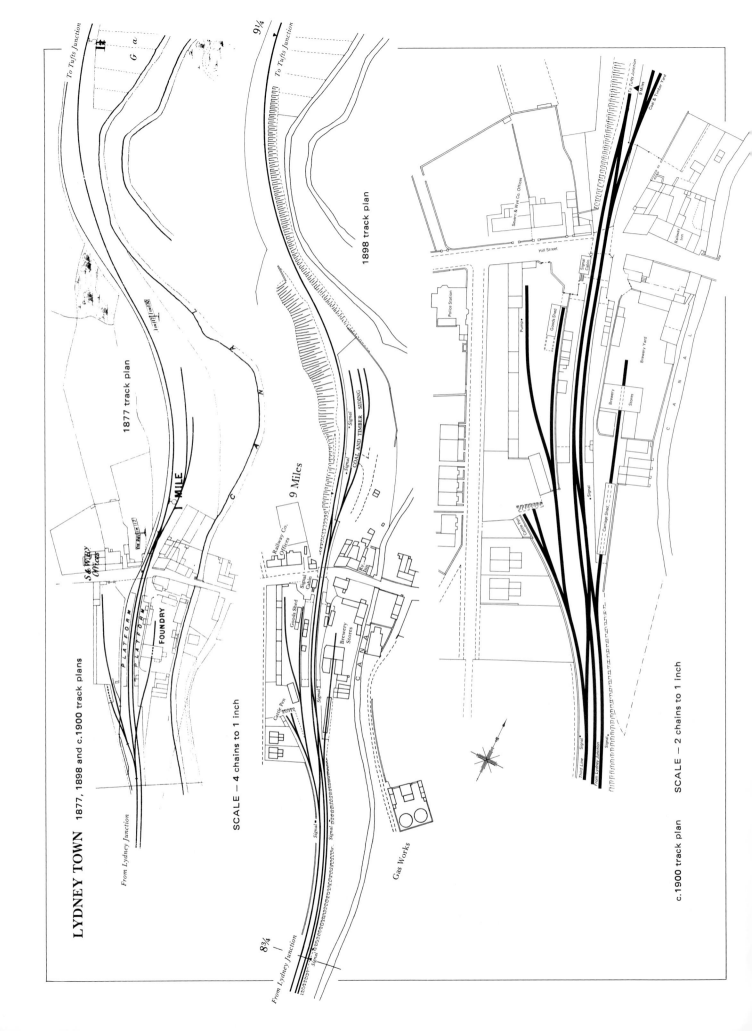

LYDNEY TOWN 1877, 1898 and c.1900 track plans

1877 track plan

To Tufts Junction

G   a

MILE

S & WYE
Offices

PLATFORM

PLATFORM

FOUNDRY

From Lydney Junction

SCALE – 4 chains to 1 inch

1898 track plan

9¾

To Tufts Junction

CANAL

9 Miles

Railway Co.
Offices

Signal Cabin

Goods Shed

Brewery
Stores

CANAL

Ry Inn

Cattle Pen

Signal

Signal

Signal

COAL AND TIMBER SIDING

Signal

Gas Works

8¾

Signal

Signal

From Lydney Junction

c.1900 track plan   SCALE – 2 chains to 1 inch

To Tufts Junction

Severn & Wye Co. Offices

Hill Street

Police Station

Pump

Goods Shed

Signal Cabin

9 Miles

Railway Inn

Brewery Yard

Brewery

Stores

Carriage Shed

Signal

Cattle Pen

Third Line   Signal

Signal

From Lydney Junction

Coal & Timber Yard

CANAL

A late 1940s view of the station with the original S & W building on the right. The furthermost portion of the structure is believed to have been a subsequent addition to Eassie's basic 20 ft building. The separate shed beyond, at the bottom of the footbridge steps, was the appointed agent's office already referred to, in use as a lamp room at this time.   *Rev. D. A. Tipper*

No. 2132 with a well patronized Berkeley auto train alongside the 'up' platform on 10th April 1945.   *V. R. Webster*

Looking south from the station footbridge on 14th April 1933. The former, presumably Great Western, wooden space and pale fencing is still in evidence here, although the 'down' main starting signal with the bracket starting signal for the mineral line is a post 1906 Midland replacement. Spare coaches for the Berkeley service have been left in the yard and Perrett's private siding can also just be discerned leading off behind the platform.   *L. E. Copeland*

Another Berkeley auto train in the 'up' platform, this time on 17th August 1956, and more unusually in the charge of one of the large wheeled '54XX' panniers.   *L. E. Copeland*

Looking west along Hill Street around the turn of the century. The Severn & Wye offices can just be seen on the right. See page 7.

Collection N. Parkhouse

A later view of the level crossing on 26th June 1948. The north end of the former agent's office is featured on the left. It appears to have started life as the superstructure of a standard 'Gloucester' signal box but no evidence has been discovered so far to indicate where it was salvaged from.

L. E. Copeland

Another view of Hill Street, this time looking east, showing the rear of the signal box and one of the flights of steps leading to the footbridge.
Collection N. Parkhouse

A double-headed train running over the crossing in the 1960s.

M. Rees

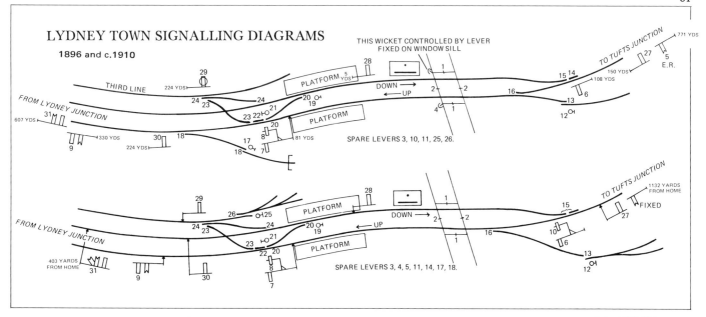

LYDNEY TOWN SIGNALLING DIAGRAMS
1896 and c.1910

THIS WICKET CONTROLLED BY LEVER
FIXED ON WINDOW SILL

TO TUFTS JUNCTION 771 YDS

THIRD LINE 224 YDS PLATFORM 5 YDS DOWN UP TO TUFTS JUNCTION

FROM LYDNEY JUNCTION 607 YDS PLATFORM 81 YDS SPARE LEVERS 3, 10, 11, 25, 26.

330 YDS 224 YDS

FROM LYDNEY JUNCTION 403 YARDS FROM HOME PLATFORM DOWN UP TO TUFTS JUNCTION 1132 YARDS FROM HOME FIXED

PLATFORM SPARE LEVERS 3, 4, 5, 11, 14, 17, 18.

In 1897 the Board of Trade requested a return of periods of actual work of the Joint Signalmen. However, although they consequently recommended that the hours at five of the cabins should be reduced from 12 to 10 hours a day, the Committee would only agree to a reduction at Lydney Town. This was because of the arduous work associated with the recently adopted method of working the gates with the wheel in the new box. Lydney Town signal box was built to a standard GWR design of the period, similar to many others all over that company's system. This particular example housed a 26 lever frame but the position of the wheel working the wicket gate was moved not long after installation following an accident on 6th December 1896. It seems that a Mrs. Wall was injured when her leg became trapped in one of the wicket gates which was being closed while she was passing through it. The wheel was repositioned so that the gates were visible when operating it. The separate wicket lever by the open window was an unusual feature.

Collection Mike Rees

Lydney viewed from Primrose Hill with a 'mixed' train hauled by an 0—6—0 saddle tank, passing the coal and timber yard at Lydney Town. Another saddle tank with three more coaches can also be seen on the third line beyond the station, together with four more coaches in the goods yard. The steeple of St. Mary's church and the chimneys of the tinplate works dominate the horizon.

Collection N. Parkhouse

Looking north from the station, showing the commencement of the single line section to Tufts Junction on 14th June 1933. The coal and timber wharf on the right also served the Lydney Central Trading Company's depot. They were general builders merchants receiving supplies of timber, slate, chimney pots, etc. A short spur siding on which to stand the timber crane was added in 1896 as considerable difficulty had been experienced in loading this traffic with the existing lines being too widely spaced. From 29th September 1898 Alfred John Thomas and John Frederick Pritchard, trading as Lydney Coal Company, took over a wharf, office and weighing machine formerly leased by F. H. Gosling, manager of LCC Wholesale & Retail Coal Factors. They received supplies of house coal for local distribution and ran their own wagon. Other coal merchants included Charles English who leased 120 sq yds from 15th October 1913, William Stephen Watts who leased 200 sq yds 'with permission to erect a shed thereon in which to store a weighing machine' and possibly Messrs. Pates & Co. who leased a 60 sq yd stacking ground from 6th November 1907.

The entrance to this yard dates from the 1896 improvements to the level crossing, the short fence and gate closing the yard from the public road being added the following year. The varying width of the roadway dictated the unequal length crossing gates shown here and on pages 79-81. They closed segmentally, i.e. one by one, rather than sympathetically, i.e. together.   *L. E. Copeland*

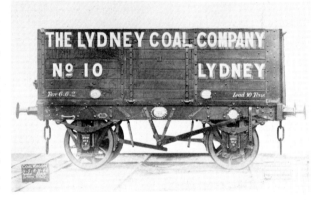

Two of Lydney Coal Company's wagons built by the Gloucester Wagon Co. and photographed in 1894 and 1899 respectively.
Gloucester Railway Carriage & Wagon Co.

An unidentified '16XX' class passing the site of Norchard Colliery on 7th September 1960.   *A. K. Pope*

MIDDLE AND UPPER FORGES AND NEW MILLS

The Middle and Upper Forges were built in the early 1600s by Sir Edward Winter to make and work iron. By 1640 the Upper Forge was being used as a slitting mill, for the purpose of cutting flat bars for use in sail making, but by 1673 it was in use again as a forge. The Winter estate was, however, heavily in debt by 1718 when Lady Frances Winter sold it to mortgagees who, in the following year, sold it to Benjamin Bathurst.

The Bathurst family leased the works to various parties until by 1800 it was held by the Pidcocks who had built the canal from Middle Forge to the River Severn. In 1814 the lease was transferred to John James who laid sidings off the tramroad into the works. The New Mills was added to the complex in 1824 to produce flat sheet for the tinplate works.

As has already been seen, the works was taken over by the Allaways in 1847 and in 1866 it was reported that with some 400 employees, about 1000 boxes of tinplate were being produced per week. In 1875 the works was transferred to R. Thomas & Co.

The tramroad between Upper Forge and Lydney Basin was retained when the broad gauge line was constructed, and still remained after its subsequent conversion to standard gauge. In 1873 a short siding to a tramroad interchange wharf at New Mills was laid, on the Wigpool Iron Ore Company's application to connect Norchard Colliery with the main line and also to effect a railway approach to the New Mills. Although this siding existed, R. Thomas & Co. continued to use the tramroad until 1883. A new length was in fact laid between Middle Forge and New Mills in 1875, on the east of the railway to avoid one of the tramroad/railway level crossings which Colonel Rich objected to in his report for the Board of Trade prior to the commencement of passenger services. The tramroad level crossing at Middle Forge was retained until March 1883 when, because of the danger to the railway, it was removed. This may have

been a ploy on behalf of the Severn & Wye to gain the removal of the remaining stretch of tramroad against the wishes of R. Thomas & Co.

In 1887 there was some debate between Thomas and the Severn & Wye over the tolls charged for carrying materials in the process of manufacture between the New Mills and the tinplate works at Lower Forge. He requested that the charge of 6d per ton be halved to compensate for the removal of the tramroad, contending that this would enable the New Mills to be kept open and the S & W would benefit from the coal traffic to the works.

The quantity of materials carried between the Upper and Lower works in the process of manufacture was, at this time, about 4,228 tons per annum, coal and other traffic to New Mills amounting to a further 5,165 tons. However, the S & W claimed that the cost of working the traffic between the two sites including time spent shunting, was 6d per ton and it would appear that the toll was not reduced.

The Upper Forge was dismantled in 1890 and was quickly followed by Middle Forge and New Mills in 1891.

As has been seen, the tramroad between Middle Forge and the Lower Forge was the cause of some dispute between R. Thomas & Co. and the Severn & Wye and this did not stop with its removal. The inhabitants of the Forest had treated the tramroads as footpaths and, after their conversion to railway, continued to treat them as such. Naturally the power and speed of a locomotive was far greater than that of a horse and so accidents to trespassers became more frequent. R. Thomas & Co. were warned repeatedly during 1893 about their employees using the line as a footpath between Middle Forge and Lydney, and in July 1894 a John Lea was run over by a train at New Mills and subsequently died in hospital. It was not until 1900 that the Joint Committee realized that there were no trespass warning signs on the Severn & Wye and erected standard pattern ones.

New Mills occupation crossing in 1956 showing the site of the 1873 interchange siding which lay between the house and the railway boundary fence. The hut by the crossing contained a telephone, which was used when timber was being hauled from Lydney Park Estate. When necessary a member of staff was posted at the crossing to handsignal such movements. He had to obtain permission from both Lydney Town and Tufts Junction signal boxes before allowing any vehicle to proceed over the crossing. Both boxes also had to be informed when the crossing was clear. It is likely that the telephone was provided in 1918 at a cost of £50. *L. E. Copeland*

KIDNALL'S SIDING

In November 1877 Mr. Simeon Holmes, a coal proprietor, and Mr. Smith, a coal factor, submitted a plan to the Severn & Wye Board showing their proposals for developing the Nags Head Colliery.

The Nags Head gale had been granted in 1846 to a Free Miner called John Beddis to gain coal from the Trenchard seam and all other seams above it. Holmes' and Smith's plan showed that the colliery could easily be served by the Forest of Dean Central Railway. However, they suggested that if the Severn & Wye offered a rate of 10d per ton instead of the normal 1/-, they would send the whole of their output onto the Severn & Wye at a point between the New Mills and Middle Forge. The estimated reserves of coal in the Nags Head and adjoining Kidnall's Colliery were 6,000,000 tons and Holmes further stated that, if the rate were reduced to 8d, he would guarantee to send 10,000 tons over the railway annually. The Severn & Wye agreed to the reduction and in December it was stated that Holmes was to put in the necessary signalling and a 500 yd. siding.

In March 1878 Holmes was ready to put traffic onto the railway, but it is likely that the siding was incomplete as agreement for the conveyance of coal was not reached with the Severn & Wye until March 1879. A plan of 1879 shows the siding curving round off the main line and crossing the River Lyd to a loading bank upon which terminated a tramway from the colliery.

An S. Holmes wagon of 1883 branded 'Empty to New Mills'.
Gloucester Railway Carriage & Wagon Co.

Following the death of Simeon Holmes in 1884, the Nags Head Colliery was worked by his grandsons, Simeon Oaks Holmes and Peter Holmes, trading as Holmes Bros., and working the 'Pillowell and Nags Head Steam Coal Collieries'.

By 1891 it would appear that the Trustees of Simeon Holmes had mortgaged the gale to a Mr. John Knowles and for a period no dead rent was paid to the Crown. Under the terms of gale grants this meant that the gale was forfeit to the Crown, and the appropriate steps were taken by the Gaveller. A Major H. E. Collins then came forward

THE NEW MILLS 1877 track plan

showing site of 1873 tramroad interchange siding

SCALE — **4 chains to 1 inch**

From Lydney

From Lydney

LEVEL

To Tufts Junction

NEW MILLS

Boundary

Parish

Gardens

NEW MILLS POND

KIDNALLS SIDING

9¾

KIDNALL'S SIDING

1898 track plan

To Tufts Junction

New Mills

SCALE — **4 chains to 1 inch**

NORCHARD COLLIERY

c.1920 track plan

From Lydney

Ground Frame

Ground Frame

Ground Frame

Cooling Tower

Power Station

Telfer Ropeway

Telfer Ropeway for Waste Removal

WASTE HEAPS

River Lyd

5

3

2

1

4

1   Level entrance
2   Haulage house
3   Screens
4   Empty wagon weighbridge
5   Loaded wagon weighbridge

To Tufts Junction

Chimney

TIMBER STACKING GROUND

*The inset (8 chains to 1 inch) shows Norchard
& Lydney power station c.1930.*

SCALE — **4 chains to 1 inch**

The northern end of Norchard Colliery loop on 26th March 1948 with Kidnall's siding dropping off to the right. Each end of the loop was worked from a ground frame unlocked by the electric train tablet. *L. E. Copeland*

and stated that he had been negotiating to purchase the Nags Head gale for some time and was preparing to work it with a heading driven from Pillowell Level. As will be seen later, Major Collins was a partner in the Dean Forest Navigation Coal & Fuel Company. His purchase of the gale evidently went through, as in July 1898 tenders were invited for sinking an air shaft for the Coal & Fuel Co. which, since 1896, had been in the hands of the Metropolitan Bank of Birmingham as mortgagees of Major Collins. A plan of this date shows that the siding by then had a loop immediately before the loading bank.

The gale was eventually surrendered to the Crown in 1903 together with the other gales once worked by the Coal & Fuel Co. and held by the Metropolitan Bank.

The siding, which had probably been disused at least since 1896, was now to serve as the access to the newly re-opened Norchard Colliery.

NORCHARD COLLIERY

Coal had been worked in this vicinity since at least 1282 under the area known as Norchard Wood, which was outside Crown land. Ownership of the land had passed in the 1700s to the Bathurst family as part of Lydney Park Estate.

A level existed on this site in 1810 when it formed part of the ironworks concern leased by the Pidcocks. In that year they were trying to dispose of their interests and the colliery was described as consisting of:

.... One Six Feet and Two Three Feet Veins of Coal, and extends over about 500 acres, and at present worked by one level and two Pits, but any more may be opened, and Works to the River Severn where the Coals sell for 12s to 14s per Ton the present price for getting the coal and delivering it to the River Severn through a private canal belonging to the works about 5s 6d per Ton. These works and Collieries are held under a lease

from the Rt. Hon. Charles Bathurst, about 67 years of which are unexpired, at the yearly rental of £250 free from Poor Rates and Tythes.'

Although the Pidcocks' interest in the ironworks was assigned back to Bathurst in 1813, it would appear that they retained an interest in the colliery as in 1814 John Pidcock was applying to the Severn & Wye to make a turnout 'from one road to the other' opposite his level at Norchard. It is possible that John Pidcock and others made a fresh start at the level in 1842, but likely that the main coal working was done through the Norchard Pit to the north-west of the level, coal probably being loaded onto the railway after 1873 on the siding at New Mills.

When in 1879 Kidnall's Siding was laid, it passed over the top of Norchard Level. It is doubtful if any work was being

A closer view of the ground frame shown in the previous view.
L. E. Copeland

Norchard Colliery viewed across the Lydney-Whitecroft road. The level crossing gates can be seen at the end of the headshunt. The chimney on the right was built in 1904 in connection with a small power station built by the Colliery Co. The timber stacking ground on the left was used for storing the timber for pit-props and served by a siding which ran across a bridge over the River Lyd.   *Collection Neil Parkhouse*

done through the level at this time and certainly the 1881 Ordnance Survey shows it as disused.

In 1890 Park Iron Mines and Collieries Limited was set up to work Norchard, and in 1891 adjoining works were assigned to the company which were later to form the eastern workings of Norchard. This company also worked the Tufts Iron Level near Tufts Junction.

In 1896 the concern was taken over by the Park Iron Ore and Coal Company Limited, the directors of which included Joseph Hale of the Lydney and Crumpmeadow Collieries Limited and the Phipps brothers who were brewers from Northampton. By 1900 it would appear that the company was being run by Richard Thomas. It is possible that when he had taken over the lease of the ironworks properties in 1871 the colliery was still included and that he had sub-let it. It was in 1900 that the company applied

to the Severn & Wye to make a second entrance into their workings under the railway, and thus probable that work was restarted through the level at this time. Use was now made of Kidnall's Siding to load the coal won and by 1903 a set of screens had been built over the siding, which then split into three roads before joining up again to form a headshunt.

Empty wagons rolled down the siding from the main line and up into the headshunt and returned by gravity through the screens to await collection. In 1904/05 a new road was built between Lydney and Whitecroft and a level crossing installed across the headshunt. Access to the siding was by means of a single connection trailing from the 'up' direction. This effectively meant that it could only be serviced by Lydney-bound trains. In practice empties from Lydney were first taken through to Tufts where the loco-

A view across the main line c.1909 showing the original set of screens built in 1906. The houses in the left background were owned by the Colliery Co. and occupied by the under manager and the engineer. The line of washing to the left of the screen belonged to a small cottage alongside.   *T. Radway*

Top: This view taken in 1923 shows the replacement set of screens built in 1921 and the conveyor to the newly constructed power station.
Above: An aerial view of the colliery and Lydney power station with the new cooling tower under construction in 1929. Telfer aerial ropeways can be seen crossing the Lydney-Whitecroft road, the nearest conveying ash from the power station and the other waste from the colliery to a tip off to the right. The houses on the right were 'all electric homes' built by the West Gloucestershire Power Co.

Collection A. K. Pope and Aerofilms

A selection of Norchard wagons.
Gloucester Railway Carriage & Wagon Co. & L. E. Copeland

motive from the north-bound train ran round them and took them back to the colliery. It returned to Tufts with loaded wagons which were left there for collection by an 'up' train.

The single line section between Lydney Town and Tufts Junction was, of course, occupied throughout the operation, thus often causing delays. This was obviated to some extent in 1906, when a loop siding was added alongside the main line, allowing the colliery to be serviced from each direction. A new siding was laid into the colliery at the same time, coming off the new loop at the southern end and running alongside the River Lyd before connecting with the original siding. A set of screens was built over the new line, empty wagons running in on the original northernmost siding down into the headshunt which now ended before the level crossing. From here they ran through the screens, over the loaded wagon weighbridge and off down the new siding to await collection. The new arrangements provided accommodation for 50 wagons.

From about 1909 the Joint Committee kept a close eye on the Norchard workings to make sure that they did not interfere with the railway by causing subsidence. Annual inspections were carried out by the Midland Railway's engineer, but certainly up to 1923 no subsidence had been noted.

A change of management took place in June 1912 when the Park Colliery Company, formed by Charles Bathurst, leased Norchard from R. Thomas & Co. Bathurst became chairman of the new company and R. Beaumont Thomas, eldest son of Richard Thomas, became one of the directors.

In 1921 a further set of screens was built over the southern siding following a fire which destroyed the 1906 set. In 1923 the West Gloucestershire Power Company built its generating station alongside Norchard together with an overhead conveyor belt to supply coal direct from the screens to the power station. Coal was also brought into the Norchard sidings from other collieries and again moved to the power station using the conveyor. A siding from the Norchard headshunt was also constructed into the power station to facilitate the movement of equipment.

The Park Colliery Company also owned several other gales which by September 1924 included Pillowell United. The boundaries of this and a neighbouring gale were rearranged to enable Pillowell coal to be worked through Norchard. In September, however, the pumps in this area failed, which led to the overpowering of the main pumps at Norchard by the end of the year. In January 1925 the water burst into the Princess Royal Colliery workings, which were adjacent to Norchard's northern boundary, and the flow of water was not finally stopped until October 1925. For the expense of pumping Princess Royal dry, £12,500 was claimed from the Park Colliery Company, plus compensation for lost production. The Commissioners of Woods were approached for financial help for Norchard which, like all of the Forest's collieries, was going through a difficult time due to poor sales. It was pointed out to them that if Norchard was forced to close, Princess Royal would undoubtedly also close due to the increased costs in keeping the pit free of water. Therefore the Crown would lose the royalties from both, plus the dead rent from Princess Royal. However, the Crown was unable to assist, as they had recently loaned money to Princess Royal and had no spare funds in their coffers. The Commissioners of Woods were then asked if they would mediate in the dispute as neither side would meet to discuss the problem, the logical answer to which was amalgamation.

In 1926 came the problem of the General Strike and this prolonged dispute between the miners and the coal owners merely dragged Norchard further into debt. By 1928 Charles Bathurst, by now Lord Bledisloe, was personally losing money each week as he felt so strongly about his miners and wanted to keep them in employment. The colliery was cleared once a day, the output at this time usually being about ten loaded wagons. In January 1930, however, an announcement was made that the statutory notice had been given to the Gaveller of the closure of the Norchard gales. It was estimated at this time that when Norchard closed, the extra pumping costs for Princess Royal would be £25,000 per year. Finally in February, agreement on amalgamation was reached, with the Princess Royal Colliery Company buying a controlling interest in Norchard from Charles Bathurst.

By 1932 a new roadway had been driven to unite the two collieries underground, to aid ventilation and other services, but, although they were physically linked, the two collieries were still worked as separate concerns.

By 1936 it was becoming obvious that coal production at Norchard was being concentrated in the Pillowell area and that coal was being hauled about three miles to the surface from the working face. It also meant that the colliers were having to walk three miles underground and their wages were paid from the time they started work at the face. This was especially hard on the men who lived in the Pillowell area as it meant they had a six mile walk to win coal from directly underneath their homes! The decision was therefore made to drive a new heading, or slant, to the surface at Pillowell. The entrance was to be known as Norchard Pillowell, or New Norchard. Driving the heading from within began in 1937 and it took about one year to reach the surface. A tree, which the surveyors had taken as their target, virtually fell into the hole as they broke through! To enable the coal raised through this new 'horizon' to be carried back to the power station, three sidings were laid on the site of the old Pillowell Level sidings which had been lifted in 1898. New screens were built and the coal was taken down the Mineral Loop to Norchard and the power station. Here it was tipped into a hopper by the old screens and taken by the conveyor system to the power station's boiler house.

A survey of Forest mines in 1946 forecast that Princess Royal and Norchard had a possible life of about one hundred years. Within ten, however, the workings on the eastern side of Norchard, towards Howbeech and Eastern United Colliery, reached thin coal and, as this was expensive to work, the decision was made to close in 1957.

The southern connection at Norchard was removed in 1948, the original northern connection being retained to enable coal to be worked into the power station. This was finally removed in 1958, when all coal for the power station was brought in by road. The sidings at Pillowell were also removed in 1958, the last load being collected in November 1957.

Norchard was peculiar in that it was the only colliery in the Forest of Dean which did not lie under Crown land,

A group of colliers at Norchard with their open carbide lamps. Forest collieries were free of gas and so open flames could be used with little risk.   *Collection A. K. Pope*

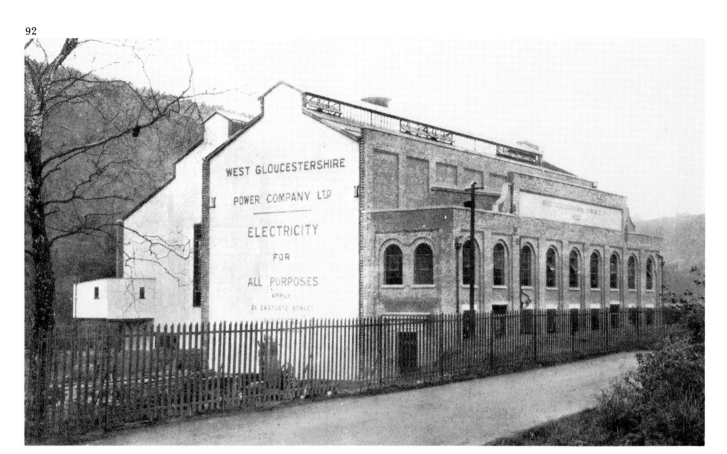

The newly completed power station. The top view shows the south end wall, which was built of corrugated iron to allow for possible extension. However, this was never needed.

Collection A. K. Pope

being situated under the Lydney Park Estate owned by the Bathurst family. At its peak it had given employment to 300-400 men and produced 1,800-2,000 tons of coal per week. However, at times 38 tons of water had to be pumped in order to win one ton of coal.

LYDNEY POWER STATION

The contract for building the power station for the West Gloucestershire Power Company was let on 18 December 1922 and by 18 June 1923 the station was in commercial operation — from digging the foundations to electricity production in just six months!

It was built alongside Norchard Colliery, partially on an old waste tip, and alongside the River Lyd, these two factors ensuring a ready supply of both coal and water. Coal was also brought into the colliery sidings from elsewhere and unloaded onto a conveyor belt system which transported the coal directly into storage bunkers above the boiler furnaces.

To aid construction and also the future movement of heavy machinery into the power station, a siding was laid which came off the colliery headshunt and ran into the station's machine room.

In 1923 the station had two generating sets capable of producing a total of 10,000 kW, and in 1928 the turbine house was further extended when another generator was added of 7,500 kW capacity. Electricity was generated on the three phase alternating system at 6,600 volts at the national frequency of 50 cycles. To enable a large area to be served, this voltage was boosted to 33,000 volts in the

The interior of the turbine room.   *Collection A. K. Pope*

nearby main transforming station, transmission lines spreading out to form a ring main around the Forest of Dean to serve all the major collieries and also domestic users. A transmission line crossed the River Severn and served the Stroud Valley, whilst others served Gloucester and Chepstow. The West Gloucestershire Power Company was later taken over by the Electricity Generating Board and then by the Midland Electricity Board. After the Norchard sidings were removed in 1958, all coal was brought in by road until the closure of the station in 1968. It was demolished in the winter of 1968/69.

The rear of the power station in later years. The wooden cooling tower was built to supplement the original and lasted until the closure of the station.
CEGB

The southern approach to Tufts Junction in the late 1950s. According to the official singling notice, the left hand arm of the former MR bracket signal applied to trains going on to the Oakwood branch, the middle arm to the siding (the former 'down' line) and the right hand arm to trains continuing on the single line. These arrangements dated from Sunday, 30th November 1930. *R. Dagley-Morris*

TUFTS JUNCTION

The establishment of a junction at Tufts dates from tramroad days when the privately-owned Dyke's tramroad, built in 1855, joined the main line here. The Kidnall's Mill branch was also reconnected here in 1856 when it was re-aligned below Pillowell to give easier curves and gradients.

In 1868, with the laying of the broad gauge alongside the tramroad, Tufts also became a railway junction, a broad gauge branch being laid alongside the Kidnall's Mill branch as far as Pillowell Level Colliery, for the accommodation of the owners of the Patent Fuel Works at Whitecroft. This was later incorporated in the route of the Mineral Loop which was opened in April 1872 as a standard gauge line, a third rail laid inside the existing track providing mixed gauge to Lydney. It was thus possible to see broad and standard gauge trains running alongside a horse-drawn tramroad on this stretch of the line, surely a rare combination. However, this situation only lasted for about a month before the entire system was converted to standard gauge.

In connection with the commencement of passenger traffic in 1875, a signal box was erected at Tufts Junction on the 'up' side in a position to allow for the proposed deviation referred to on page 5. Unfortunately, no details of this structure have so far come to light, but in 1889 the discovery of a discrepancy in the railway boundary at this point revealed that it had been built partly on land owned by Mr. Bathurst. An agreement was subsequently reached over an adjustment of the boundary and a cottage for the signalman was also built at this time.

The junction underwent considerable change with the doubling of the line northwards to Parkend in 1897. The revised layout was controlled by a 30 lever frame housed in a new signal box built to a standard GW design similar to those also provided at Lydney Town, Whitecroft and Travellers Rest.

THE OAKWOOD BRANCH

The Oakwood branch was laid on the course of Dyke's Tramroad, which was built during 1855-56 by Thomas Dyke, to serve a level he was opening. Dyke prepared the earthworks and the Severn & Wye provided the tramplates. Under this agreement the tramroad was conveyed to the Severn & Wye in 1870 and they converted it to a railway as and when required. It was not until 1892 that it reached its final length, but in 1872 it had been part of a much grander plan when it was proposed to use the course of the Oakwood branch to make a junction railway to Milkwall. This scheme, however, was never carried out and the branch did not in fact reach the point to which it was authorized.

The first portion of the tramroad was converted in 1870, when a broad gauge siding was laid to serve a loading bank at Tufts. This bank was used for the transhipment of iron-ore with two mine tramways running onto it at different levels. The upper level was used by a tramway from the South Oakwood Iron Mine, whilst a tramway from the Tufts

An earlier view looking back towards Lydney on 14th April 1933. The line furthest from the camera was the up loop, effectively the end of the Mineral Loop, the centre track was the former up main in use as a single running line by this time and the one in the foreground was the former down main in use as a siding. The trap points and ground signal at the end of the siding were provided when the line was singled. According to a 1929 signalling diagram, the two up starting signals on the left replaced a bracket signal.   *L. E. Copeland*

Iron Level, which belonged to the Park Iron Ore & Coal Company, the owners of Norchard Colliery, ran onto the bank at the lower level. In 1897 the Park Iron Ore & Coal Co. were given permission to erect a shed over the sidings and loading bank. Both tramways were out of use by 1920 but some traffic was still loaded at the bank until 1948, from a small wood distillation works situated nearby.

Wood distillation works were set up in various parts of the Forest from about 1835 and the one at Tufts was the

last, beginning operation in 1887. They were established to use poor quality or brush wood which would otherwise be wasted. This had previously been used to make charcoal for use in the iron furnaces, but by the 1830s coke was beginning to supersede charcoal in iron making, thus leaving a surplus of wood. In the distillation works charcoal was produced in order to gain its by-products. The resulting gases from the charcoal-making process were drawn off into condensation vessels, from which the resultant products

No. 1626 arriving at Tufts Junction with empties for Princess Royal on 8th June 1962.   *R. Dagley-Morris*

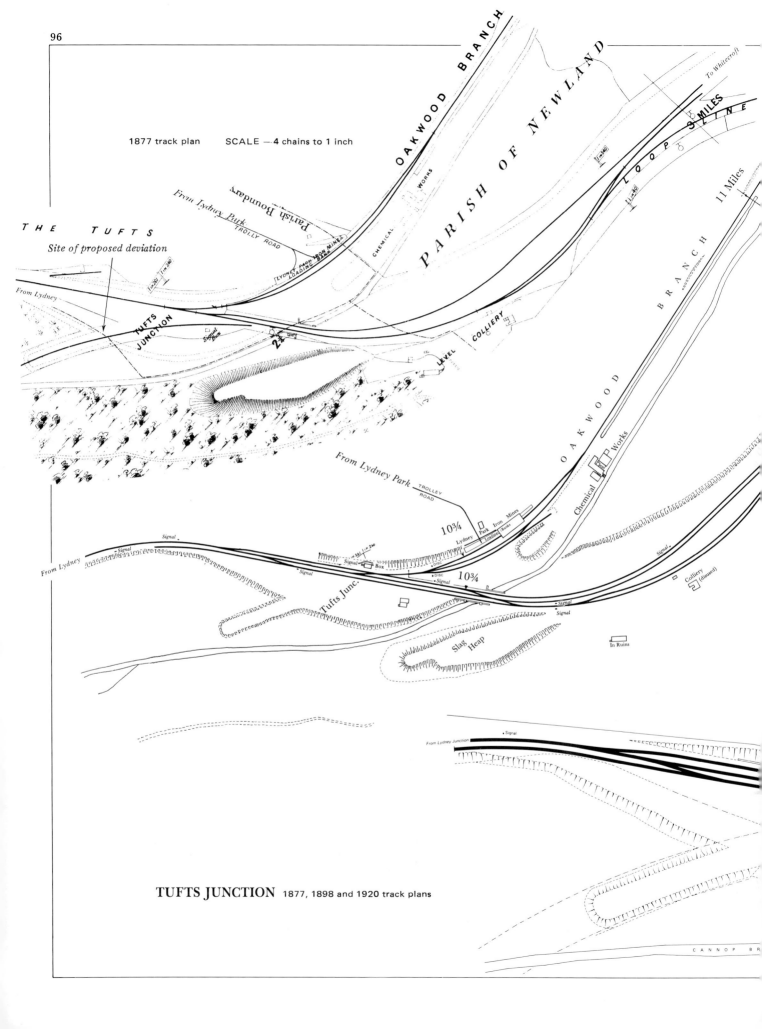

OAKWOOD BRANCH

PARISH OF NEWLAND

To Whitecroft

1877 track plan   SCALE — 4 chains to 1 inch

LOOP 3 MILES LINE

11 Miles

THE TUFTS

Site of proposed deviation

From Lydney Park

Parish Boundary

TROLLY ROAD

WORKS

CHEMICAL

LYDNEY PARK IRON MINES

LOADING BANK

From Lydney

TUFTS JUNCTION

1 in 240

1 in 240

Signal Box

COLLIERY

LEVEL

O A K W O O D   B R A N C H

Chemical Works

From Lydney Park

TROLLEY ROAD

10¾   Park Iron Mines

Lydney   Loading Bank

Signal

Signal

Signal

1 in 240

Signal

Tufts Junc.

Signal   Box

DISC

10¾

Signal

Signal

Colliery (disused)

Signal

In Ruins

Slag   Heap

From Lydney Junction   Signal

TUFTS JUNCTION 1877, 1898 and 1920 track plans

CANNOP BR

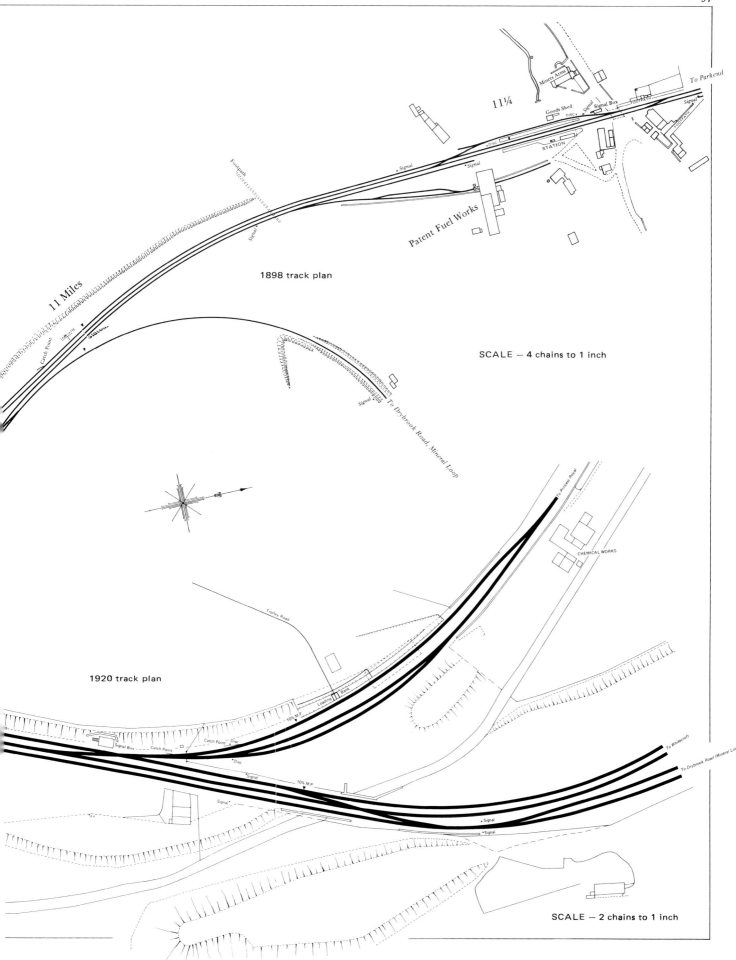

11 Miles

11¼

To Parkend

Miners Arms

Goods Shed

Signal Box

STATION

Patent Fuel Works

Footpath

Signal

Catch Point

To Drybrook Road, Mineral Loop

1898 track plan

SCALE — 4 chains to 1 inch

To Princess Royal

CHEMICAL WORKS

Trolley Road

1920 track plan

Loading Bank

10½ M P

Signal Box

Catch Point

Disc

To Whitecroft

To Drybrook Road (Mineral Loop)

10½ M P

Signal

Signal

SCALE — 2 chains to 1 inch

Looking north this time, with the Oakwood branch diverging through the gate beyond the signal box. The smaller arm on the right of the down starting signal applied to trains bound for the Mineral Loop. The signalman's cottage of 1889 is featured on the right of this view taken on 8th June 1962 and may be seen in greater detail on page 20. *R. Dagley-Morris*

were pyroligneous acid and tar. At Tufts the tar was pumped into wooden barrels and dispatched by rail. The acid was further processed, passing through stills from which emerged naptha, to which lime was added, and the whole was boiled until solidification took place. This produced acetate of lime which was dug out and bagged up for sale.

The works at Tufts were started by Isaac Jacobs who, in 1887, was granted permission to use an existing gateway in the railway fence in order to unload materials on the site. After several changes of ownership it closed in 1913, when

the lessees were Thomas Newcomen and John Capel, who had taken over the lease in 1905 and also owned the chemical works at Lydbrook. The same lessees re-opened the works in 1917 and two years later were authorized by the Joint Committee to extend the loading bank. The works continued in production until 1948 when they were dismantled.

About 100 yards north north-east of the works described above, and on the opposite side of the Oakwood branch, stood the Whitecroft Chemical Works. Unfortunately, little

Tufts Junction signal box on 5th February 1965, a standard GW structure. *A. K. Pope*

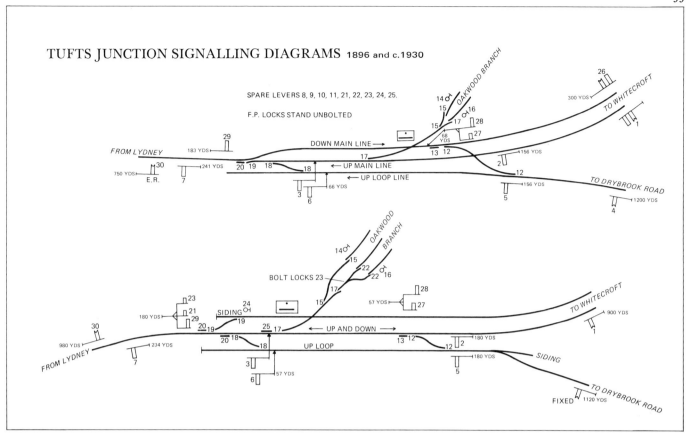

TUFTS JUNCTION SIGNALLING DIAGRAMS 1896 and c.1930

SPARE LEVERS 8, 9, 10, 11, 21, 22, 23, 24, 25.

F.P. LOCKS STAND UNBOLTED

OAKWOOD BRANCH

TO WHITECROFT

FROM LYDNEY 183 YDS DOWN MAIN LINE →

300 YDS

26

68 YDS

29

E.R. 750 YDS 30 241 YDS 7 ← UP MAIN LINE

← UP LOOP LINE

66 YDS 3 6

TO DRYBROOK ROAD 1200 YDS 4

156 YDS

156 YDS

OAKWOOD BRANCH

BOLT LOCKS 23

TO WHITECROFT

SIDING 24

23 21 29 180 YDS 57 YDS

FROM LYDNEY 980 YDS 30 234 YDS 7 ← UP AND DOWN →

UP LOOP 57 YDS

900 YDS 1

180 YDS

SIDING

FIXED 1120 YDS *TO DRYBROOK ROAD*

The interior of Tufts Junction signal box with signalman Archie Rowe. This is one of the few views featuring a Tyers No. 6 tablet instrument (in the foreground) which is used here to control the Tufts Junction to Lydney Town section. The right hand view shows the miniature staff instrument which controlled the Tufts-Parkend section after the 1930 singling.

A. K. Pope

The signalman's view of a loaded train arriving back at Tufts Junction from Princess Royal on 5th February 1965.

A. K. Pope

is known about this concern. It was in existence in 1876 when it was listed in a trade directory as 'Messrs. Chapman & Morgan, Chemical Manufacturers', and in the same year Mr. Morgan applied to the Severn & Wye for permission to construct an access road over the Oakwood branch near Park Hill. The date of closure is also uncertain, a Severn & Wye minute of August 1883 stating that a Mr. David Harries of Whitecroft Chemical Works was in arrears with his account and that he was in fact closing his works. Trade directories, however, still list M. Morgan & Co. as owners in 1887 and 1891. A siding to a loading wharf served the works, but in 1906 it was reported in the Joint Committee's minute books as having not been used for a considerable time and, as it needed renewal, it was decided to lift the rails.

In 1874 the branch was extended to Park Hill Level which was served by three sidings terminating at a loading wharf onto which ran a tramway direct from the mouth of the level.

Park Hill was galed in 1825 to a free miner by the name of John Hawkins who leased it to David Mushet, the famed metallurgist, who owned iron works in the district and required a supply of iron ore. By December 1857 the lease of the gale had passed to Mushet's son William, who in that month leased it to the Park Hill Colliery Company.

Although Park Hill was an iron mine, it also contained four seams of coal which were separately galed in 1845, and in 1858 it was reported that the Park Hill Mining Company Dean Forest Limited were the owners of two gales — Park Hill Colliery and Park Hill Iron Mine. In November 1858 it was stated that the collieries had been unproductive and had been shut up for some years. Subsequently the whole property passed to the Dean Forest Iron Company which was owned by the Crawshay family who were large coal and iron proprietors within the Forest. The coal level was

relinquished by Henry Crawshay & Sons in 1896, although they continued to work the iron mine through an adjoining gale until that too was relinquished to the Crown in July 1922.

Park Hill coal gale was re-allocated in April 1916 and was known as Park Hill No. 2 Colliery. The lessee was Henry Etherington Doughty, but it would appear that the venture was not a success as the sidings were removed in 1919, having already been reduced to two by 1898. By the end of 1921 the lease was in the hands of C. A. Morgan who was in the process of mortgaging it to E. J. & T. W. Thomas. They in turn conveyed it to the Wilda Collieries Ltd. of Ashby-de-la-Zouch, Leicestershire, who already owned several other gales in the area. It is possible that the sidings were relaid at this period as the 1922 Ordnance Survey shows one siding and a tramway running from the level. The colliery was again disused by 1930 and the gale was forfeited in August 1932 for non-payment of the dead rent to the Crown, the sidings finally being removed in 1935.

In order to ease traffic working to the Princess Royal Colliery, at the end of the Oakwood branch, a loop was laid in at the Park Hill sidings in 1907. Prior to this, empties were propelled up the branch, the locomotive running round the train using the main line at Tufts, thus delaying other traffic. Running round was subsequently carried out at Park Hill from where the wagons were then propelled to Princess Royal.

In 1876 the railway was extended about 200 yards further along the Dyke's tramroad to Dyke's (or Whitecroft) Level which had a siding and a loading bank on the 'up' side. The Severn & Wye were approached to carry out the extension but they could not afford it. Captain Walter Ross, the owner of Princess Royal Gale, of which Dyke's Level was a part, advanced the Severn & Wye £500 to carry out

No. 4671 propelling wagons to Princess Royal passing the site of Morgan's chemical works on the right in October 1964.   *R. Marrows*

The remains of Tufts loading bank in June 1962. The two levels are just discernible and the building to the right of the photograph was part of Morgan's Chemical Works.
R. Dagley-Morris

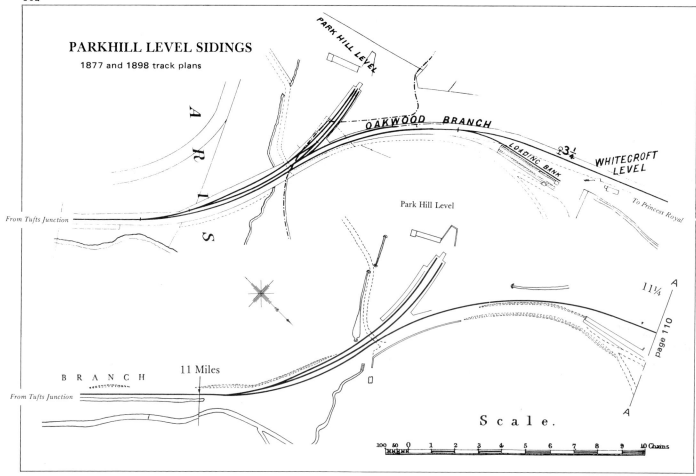

PARKHILL LEVEL SIDINGS
1877 and 1898 track plans

PARK HILL LEVEL

OAKWOOD BRANCH

LOADING BANK

3¼ WHITECROFT LEVEL

To Princess Royal

Park Hill Level

From Tufts Junction

11¼

page 110

11 Miles

BRANCH

From Tufts Junction

A

A

Scale.

100 50 0 1 2 3 4 5 6 7 8 9 10 Chains

The southern end of Park Hill Loop in 1961. *J. Dagley-Morris*

No. 1642 propelling a brake van at Park Hill loop on 19th April 1961. *R. Dagley-Morris*

the extension. This was repaid in the form of reduced traffic rates. The history of Dyke's Level is dealt with later under Princess Royal Colliery. Suffice it to say here that the siding was removed by 1898.

In 1890-91 the branch was extended to the Park Gutter Pits which were being opened up by the Princess Royal Colliery Company. This extension also involved the alteration of the public level crossing at Park Hill Level, as it was stated that with the increased traffic on the branch, the existing crossing would be a danger. This was the limit to which the Oakwood branch was laid, although the Act of 1872 had authorized its construction as far as the Oakwood Chemical Works and also the junction railway from Knockley Gate to Milkwall.

Special regulations applied to the working of the branch and the following is an extract from the 1911 Appendix:

In working over this Branch, Engine-Drivers must proceed cautiously and be prepared to stop at any point short of any obstructions, the Line being unfenced.

Gates are fixed at Park Hill Level Crossing, the normal position of which will be across the Railway closed against the running line, and Drivers must be prepared to pull up before reaching them, travelling in either direction and on approaching the level crossing give three distinct whistles.

The Signal Porter from Whitecroft Station, when not otherwise arranged, must be at Tufts Junction each morning and evening on arrival of the Trains which go to Princess Royal Colliery, and assist there with the shunting and then go to Park Hill Level Crossing in advance of the Train and open the gates to allow it to pass to the Colliery, remaining there to protect the crossing until the Train returns and after it has passed over the level crossing secure the gates in their normal position, returning the key to the Signalman on duty at Tufts Junction Signal Box.

The northern end of Park Hill loop on 21st January 1961. Park Hill sidings went off to the right behind the P.W. hut.   *J. Dagley-Morris*

A train passing Park Hill loop on 24th October 1962.   *R. Marrows*

The pit head at Park Gutter. The building on the right housed the electric winding engine. *R. Dagley-Morris*

PRINCESS ROYAL COLLIERY

Princess Royal was first galed on 15th June 1842 to four brothers by the name of Priest, all of whom were free miners. They in turn assigned it in November to a Mr. Morpeth. By October 1855 the deeds had been transferred to Thomas Dyke. It was stated that he had begun to drive a level into the upper coal measures of the Princess Royal gale, seeking the Yorkley seam, and he applied to the Crown for permission to build a tramroad from the level to the main line of the Severn & Wye at Tufts.

The lower coal measures were leased by Dyke to William Mullinger Higgins in March 1856. These consisted of the Whittington and Coleford High Delf seams and in July 1857 the Bristol and Forest of Dean Coal Company, with which Higgins appears to have been connected, wrote to the Crown offices expressing their desire to sink shafts and erect steam engines on land alongside the Whitecroft to

No. 1623 propelling empties into Princess Royal Colliery.
R. Dagley-Morris

Looking back down the Oakwood branch from the Park Gutter pits of the Princess Royal Colliery. The bricks on the right were from the Princess Royal brickworks.

L. E. Copeland

Looking towards the screens with the winding house on the left. The building on the right originally housed the company's offices.

A. K. Pope

No. 4671 crossing the Bream-Whitecroft road at Park Gutter in October 1964. *R. Marrows*

Bream road. They also requested permission to construct a tramroad to join that laid by Dyke.

In October 1857 the Bristol and Forest of Dean Coal Company informed the Crown that they were contemplating building three engine houses, a boiler house, an office and stores, a blacksmith's shop, a carpenter's shop and a stable and shed. In December they wanted to add some miners' cottages and sought permission to dig clay on their land to enable them to make bricks. There was, however, some difficulty in the Crown issuing leases for the above as the company were not the registered owners of the gale and consent for the works had to be gained from Dyke. The consent to dig clay was finally obtained in March 1859, although there still appears to have been problems over the main lease as the Crown refused permission for the engine houses and warned that the buildings constructed already might have to be removed.

In July 1863 the Crown increased the royalty rate for Princess Royal to 3d per ton. The gale was by now held by the Reverend William Dyke and his brother Henry who were trustees of the estate of the late Thomas Dyke. William Dyke thought that this increase of 50% was unreasonable, pointing out that the Yorkley seam could not be worked to any large extent in a profitable way. The other two seams of the gale had not yet been cut although a large sum of money had been expended. He also pointed out that the whole of the works was at a stand and entirely unproductive. The Crown in reply stated that Dyke was in fact letting the two lower seams to the Bristol and Forest of Dean Coal Company for £400 per year plus 8d per ton on all coal raised. Furthermore, he was letting a portion of the Yorkley seam to a Samuel Morgan at £240 per year plus a tonnage rate. Dyke countered claiming that he was removing the tramplates from the mouth of the level, having abandoned any idea of profitable working. He was

Looking through the screens from the level crossing towards the empty wagon sidings. *M. Rees*

also going to take the tonnage matter to arbitration, but the Crown won the day and the rate stayed at 3d!

In early 1864 when the Bristol and Forest of Dean Coal Company was being wound up by the Court of Chancery, William Dyke stated that he would like the lower measures to be surrendered to the Crown and that he would then apply for a fresh lease on them. By March 1866 the Princess Royal gale was in the hands of Messrs. Francis and Brain, and in 1874 it was owned by the United Colliery Company whose manager was a Mr. Dunning. They wished to lay a line of tramroad from Dyke's Level to a siding off the Severn & Wye main line near Whitecroft, but the Crown refused permission. However, as has been seen, in 1876

The empty wagon roads at Park Gutter on 30th April 1962.   *R. Dagley-Morris*

the Severn & Wye extended their Oakwood branch further
along the course of Dyke's tramway to Dyke's Level, now
also known as Whitecroft Level. At this time Captain Ross
was the sole owner of Princess Royal gale, but by 1888 the
ownership of it had changed hands yet again and it was now
owned by William Camm of Bream, who in September of
that year sold it to Richard Watkins, also of Bream.

FLOUR MILL COLLIERY

Flour Mill was first galed on 4th August 1843 to William
Jones, who applied to the Crown for a lease of 1½ acres
adjoining a site for a colliery for the purpose of erecting
buildings and apparatus. By 23rd August, however, it would
appear that he had disposed of his interest to George Skipp.
This worried the Crown's deputy surveyor who believed
that Skipp intended building a chemical works on the site
and feared the possible pollution of the stream. The main
reason for his concern was probably that the stream ran
past his house in Parkend! The chemical works was built by
1844, but the pollution is not recorded.

It would appear that the dead rent on the Flour Mill
gale was not paid for some time, possibly because Skipp
was not interested in the minerals. In April 1859 the gale
was put up for auction at the Feathers Hotel in Lydney,
but the bidding, however, did not reach the reserve price
and the sale did not go through. New owners had been
found by May 1864, these being Messrs. Ralph and Arthur
James Price of London, who applied for a licence of 2 acres
of land. The Crown surveyor thought this to be a large area
of land for a colliery, but was informed by the Prices that
this was the smallest area on which they were advised they
could erect engine houses for the pumping machines and
winding engines, forges, stables, carpenters' shops, tip
ground and other accommodation needed to work the
colliery on 'the very large scale' they intended. The lease
was granted from 24th June 1864 for a term of 31 years
at a rent of £5 per annum.

Looking the opposite way to the previous view, back through the
screens. The state of the colliery yard trackwork can be clearly seen,
explaining the large number of wagon derailments dealt with by the
Lydney breakdown train.   *R. Dagley-Morris*

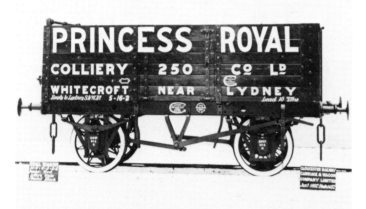

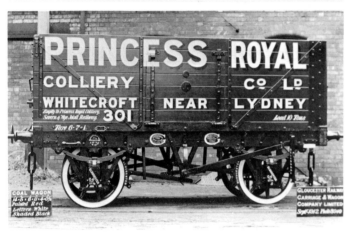

In 1870 the owners applied to lay a tramroad connection to the Oakwood Tramway.

In March 1876 the Crown's attention was drawn to an accumulation of water in two of the pits, known as Park Gutter, in the deep gale of the Princess Royal Colliery. This had been allowed to rise above the level of the workings to the injury of the Flour Mill Colliery, on the land side of the Princess Royal gale, and the Crown was requested to 'cause such water to be removed by the galee of Princess Royal Colliery'.

In November 1877 the Flour Mill gale was being assigned to Mr. W. Fowler, but it would appear that he did not carry out any further development, as in early 1882 an inquiry was made to the Gaveller as to whether any work was being carried out following the terms of the gale grant. In May ownership passed to Mr. Chapman, executor of Fowler's will, and as work had not restarted by September, the gale was forfeited to the Crown.

By November 1886 Flour Mill had passed to William Camm and Richard Watkins, owners of Princess Royal, who were anxious to open the colliery but not prepared to install expensive pumping equipment immediately. Instead Watkins proposed to drain the collieries by continuing to drive the old Dyke's (Whitecroft) Level to the Whittington seam.

PRINCESS ROYAL COLLIERY COMPANY LIMITED

On 9th March 1891 a new company, the Princess Royal Colliery Company Limited, was set up to run both Flour Mill and Princess Royal, the new owners being Sir William Marling, Frederick Winterbothom and Richard Watkins. By 1894 they had acquired other surrounding gales including Prince of Wales, Ellwood and a portion of the Parkend Deep Level Colliery.

In 1890-91 the Oakwood branch was extended from Dyke's Level to a loading bank alongside the Park Gutter pits, and a rope-worked tramway was laid from Flour Mill to enable coal to be brought down to the new screens being built there. In 1896 the Severn & Wye Co.'s fence, which lay between the colliery company's tramway and the railway sidings, was moved to the far side of the tramway as materials being loaded over the fence had damaged it!

When in 1897 the company began to raise coal through the Park Gutter shafts, it became necessary to lay extra siding accommodation at the end of the Oakwood branch to deal with the anticipated extra 300-500 tons of coal per day. The sidings were further altered in 1902 when a weighing machine was also installed.

Flour Mill Colliery was working the coal from the bottom of the shaft, which was 190 yards deep, upwards towards its western boundary, almost to the outcrop of the seam. In 1904 it therefore became necessary to sink a new shaft, 140 yards deep and fourteen feet in diameter, which enabled the company to develop the dip of the seam. The area they were working in, however, proved to be very heavily watered and required the pumping of up to 3,000 gallons per minute. Later considerable geological difficulties were met and it became necessary for yet another shaft to be sunk. As will be seen later, this was overcome by deepening the shaft at Park Gutter.

A selection of Princess Royal Colliery Co. Ltd. wagons together with one of Jarrett's branded 'empty to Princess Royal Colliery S & W Joint Railway'. Jarrett was a coal factor from Bream.
Gloucester Railway Carriage & Wagon Co.

A view across the Bream-Whitecroft road showing the building layout at Park Gutter. The red brick building on the left housed the later offices. In latter years pit head baths were provided at the larger collieries. Here they were situated just off the right hand side of the picture. This photograph was taken on the last day of operation.

A. K. Pope

Soon after the passing of the Forest of Dean (Mines) Act of 1904, several gales were amalgamated to be worked by the Princess Royal Company. These included Flour Mill, Princess Royal, Rising Sun Engine, Venus and Jupiter, Union, and the Prince of Wales, all of which were already owned by the company. They also acquired High Delf Engine, Royal, Beaufort Engine, Skinners Garden and part of New United Deep No. 1. All of the barriers within this area were to be abolished and a barrier of coal 30 yards wide was to be left all the way round the new perimeter. Barriers had to be left between adjacent properties as a form of protection, both from influxes of water and encroachment by the adjoining works. The dead rent for the whole of the new area was £1,200 per annum, but the royalty remained at 3d per ton. The company were to drive a dipple and a parallel airway forward in a straight line to the deepest part of the Coleford High Delf seam within their area. To enable them to do this, the Crown were to give financial assistance for pumping equipment if any undue quantity of water was encountered.

In 1905 the company reported that the Yorkley seam in the Park Gutter pits was being worked at a continuing loss, and they were only kept open for pumping purposes in order to keep the High Delf seam free of water at Flour Mill.

In 1906 increasing traffic from Princess Royal made further extensions to the siding accommodation necessary. The loaded wagon road was extended to hold 50 vehicles, the screen roads were altered to provide an extra machine for weighing empties, and the empty wagon road was extended to hold 51. The three empty wagon storage sidings were also

A closer view of the headframe erected in 1914, also featuring the steel tubs in which coal and waste was brought to the surface.

Collection Peter Ball

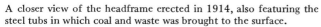

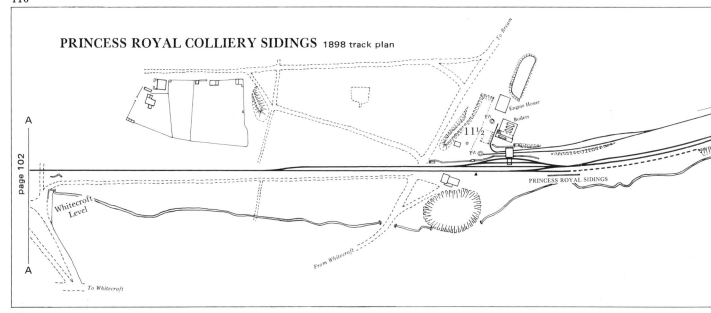

PRINCESS ROYAL COLLIERY SIDINGS 1898 track plan

lengthened to give a capacity of 96, and all of these alterations were completed in 1908.

Flour Mill Colliery suffered from a strike in October 1909 and the pit ponies were put up for sale. It lasted less than a month, but a more serious strike was the national one of 1912. It was after this that the decision was made to start work on the deepening of the Park Gutter shaft to assist the winning of coal from Flour Mill, and to open up new areas of the Coleford High Delf as laid out in the 1904 Act. Work commenced in stripping all of the old equipment out of the shaft in October 1913. A new headframe was erected and new boilers installed in 1914, and on 12th August the following year the shaft reached the Coleford High Delf seam at a depth of 205 yards. From the bottom a main dipple was driven, as per the terms of the 1904 agreement, until an overall depth of 1,500 feet below the surface was reached. Coal from the Yorkley and Coleford seams was then raised through this pit.

Flour Mill and Park Gutter were connected underground in early 1916 to provide efficient ventilation and to enable the start of coal production on a larger scale. Some coal was still being brought up the middle shaft at Flour Mill until

A postcard view of the Flour Mill pits. The rows of tubs are on the rope-worked tramway to Park Gutter. Those in the centre are lying on their sides for the greasing of wheels and axles.

Collection A. K. Pope

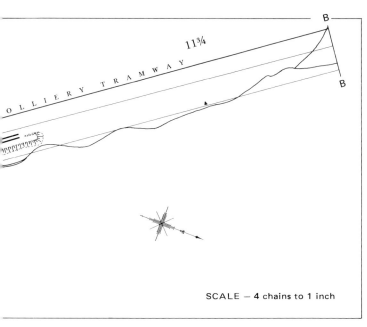

SCALE — 4 chains to 1 inch

1928, a peculiarity here being that the cages in the shaft were small and pit ponies had to sit on their haunches when entering them to be let down the shaft.

A scheme was mooted by the Princess Royal management in 1914 to build a works for converting coal into fuel oil, smokeless fuel and various by-products for use by the navy. This was to be built on Crown land alongside the tramway to Flour Mill. Negotiations with the Crown, who were worried about environmental damage, continued for several years, but eventually the idea was abandoned.

In 1922 the company erected new screens which, however, encroached upon Severn & Wye land, and for which no agreement had been reached. Although the Joint Committee consented to their remaining, subject to a suitable agreement being entered into, it was discovered that the screens had insufficient clearance to allow the passage of box vans containing stores for the colliery.

The Princess Royal management, showing considerable nerve, approached the Joint Committee with a request to contribute towards the cost of additional siding accommodation, to enable such vans to be dealt with and improve the general working arrangements. The Committee, not surprisingly, decided that the accommodation was solely for the convenience of the colliery company, and declined to assist.

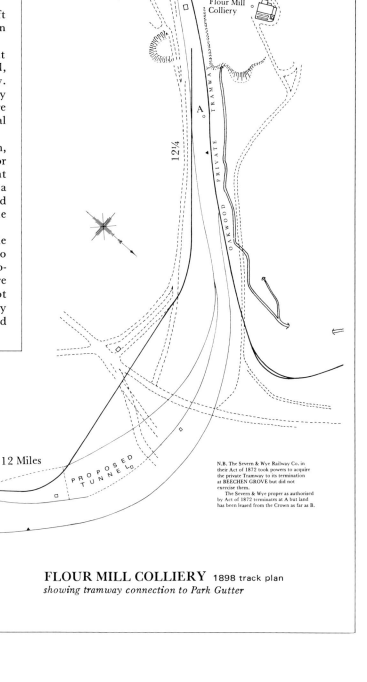

N.B. The Severn & Wye Railway Co. in their Act of 1872 took powers to acquire the private Tramway to its termination at BEECHEN GROVE but did not exercise them.
The Severn & Wye proper as authorised by Act of 1872 terminates at A but land has been leased from the Crown as far as B.

FLOUR MILL COLLIERY 1898 track plan
showing tramway connection to Park Gutter

SCALE — 4 chains to 1 inch

112

A good view of Flour Mill Colliery. The lightweight headframe on the right served the pumping shaft and was only used to remove the pump rods if necessary. The next headframe served the original winding shaft whilst the taller one beyond was that added in 1904.

Collection N. Parkhouse

Another view of Flour Mill taken before the sinking of the new shaft in 1904. This again shows clearly the tubs full of coal emerging from the shaft past the checkweighman's hut.
Collection N. Parkhouse

As already mentioned, water from Norchard burst into Princess Royal in 1925, and the company became involved in legal disputes with their neighbours. This also raised the question of the amalgamation of the two concerns. In 1930 the Princess Royal Colliery Company purchased a controlling interest in Norchard from Lord Bledisloe. This enabled the whole of the southern area of the coalfield to be worked more economically, especially after the New Norchard slant had been driven to the surface at Pillowell in 1937.

In 1938 the steam winding engine at Park Gutter was replaced by an electric one, all of the pumping underground also being electrically powered, with the capacity to deal with 5,000 gallons per minute in winter. The average quantity of water pumped was 2,700 gallons per minute, which was equivalent to 20 tons of water for each ton of coal produced. In the 1930s the annual output of coal from the Coleford High Delf was about 300,000 tons.

When in 1944 the New Fancy Colliery closed, Princess Royal was able to find employment for most of the 300 workmen. In 1953 work was restarted in the Yorkley seam, but due to bad conditions was stopped again in April 1958. In 1955 it had been decided to drive another road between Princess Royal and Norchard, which had already been united in 1932 for ventilation purposes and other services. This new link was to be a rock heading, 1,778 yards long, off which it was intended to open up a large area of the

A group of colliers at Flour Mill with the 1904 wooden headframe prominent behind. The man in the middle is wearing 'yorks', leather straps outside his trousers to stop dust travelling up his legs!
Collection N. Parkhouse

Returning to Tufts Junction, this view was taken on 14th April 1933. After the singling, the bracketed post, bearing the down starting signal for the main line and Mineral Loop respectively, remained alongside the former down main, thereafter applying to the adjacent running line. Certainly by this time all the signals at Tufts were standard Midland equipment. *L. E. Copeland*

Coleford High Delf seam in the Howbeech area towards Eastern United. Coal faces were also being driven northwards towards Cannop Colliery, which closed in 1960. However, bad conditions met in several areas, together with increased pumping costs caused by the closure of Cannop, forced the decision to close.

Final closure took place on Friday, 30th March 1962, although some coal was still screened at Park Gutter from the re-opened Pillowell shaft until 1965. This coal was brought in by road and created enough traffic for two or three outward trains per week. Part of Princess Royal was opened up to pump water from the Pillowell area, but in 1965 the cables in the Park Gutter shafts were cut and the cages allowed to fall to the bottom.

At its peak, Princess Royal had employed 1,300 men and had an output of up to 1,000 tons per day.

A closer view of the skew plate girder bridge spanning Cannop Brook and featured in the previous view.
R. Marrows

Looking north through the station c.1910, showing the new 'down' platform and shelter, extended station building and replacement brick-built urinal. The original 'up' platform extended as far as the level crossing in the background. The signal box, which can just be seen behind the shelter, was a standard GWR design of the 1890s. It was provided when the line was doubled by the Joint Committee, and housed a 30 lever frame (22 in use and 8 spare). The down inner home, again of GWR origin, is shown painted in the distinctive Midland style with a white roundel on a Markeaton red arm. At this period the finial and post would be painted lemon chrome, with the lower four feet in Venetian red. It is quite likely that the signal box would also have been painted in these colours as a result of the Midland's responsibility for signalling on this part of the line after 1906. The resulting ensemble would certainly have introduced a dash of colour into the scene! Also in view on the extreme right of the picture is a standard Midland 'rustic' platform seat which may have been painted chocolate with white lined ultramarine blue name panel on the top plank, whilst Midland platform lamps are also in evidence.   *Collection N. Parkhouse*

WHITECROFT

Whitecroft station was originally provided with just a simple platform on the 'up' side of the single running line, adjacent to the level crossing. It was provided with one of Eassie's basic wooden station buildings and a separate urinal. There do not appear to have been any goods facilities, although it is possible that some loading may have been carried out in a long loop line which extended from Tufts Junction to serve the Patent Fuel Works behind the station. However, a goods shed, a standard Gloucester Wagon Co. product, was provided in 1890 which indicates the existence of a siding by that time.

When the line was doubled between Tufts and Parkend, the work was carried out in two stages, first from Tufts to Whitecroft and then on to Parkend. This brought about a considerable change to the station and consequent improvements. A second platform was provided alongside the new running line behind which the goods yard and goods shed were served by a loop siding. The revised layout was controlled from a new 30 lever signal box which also housed a gate wheel to control the new level crossing gates.

The new platform was only 2 ft 6 ins high, presumably to match the original, but did not comply with the Board of Trade regulations. The inspecting officer also criticised it for only having an overhang of 4 inches and not being

provided with a shelter. The existing platform was 'moved' further south to fall opposite the new one, an extension at the south end replacing a portion removed from the other end, which left the station building offset.

The Board of Trade inspection was carried out on 20th November 1897, but the inspecting officer was not at all impressed with the existing accommodation, reporting:

'there is only a small wooden shed which acts as waiting room, booking office and telegraph office. The urinal is an old wooden structure and is in an unsavoury condition, and there is no waiting or retiring room for ladies. Parkend station remains unaltered and the accommodation is in much the same condition as at Whitecroft. I am unable to regard either of these stations as satisfactory, and the company should be pressed to improve the accommodation at both places within six months. They should at the same time be reminded new platforms should, as a rule, have a height of 3 ft and an overhang of 12 inches.'

The improvements, estimated to cost £224, were not completed until October 1899 and included a shelter on the 'down' platform, an extension to the existing building to give a waiting room, ladies room, 'proper conveniences for both sexes', and a corrugated iron lamp hut.

A bridleway had been built alongside the railway between Whitecroft and Parkend in 1870. It was built by the railway company on behalf of the Crown under an agreement of 3rd May. The right of way beside the line nearer to the station took the form of a pathway alongside the running

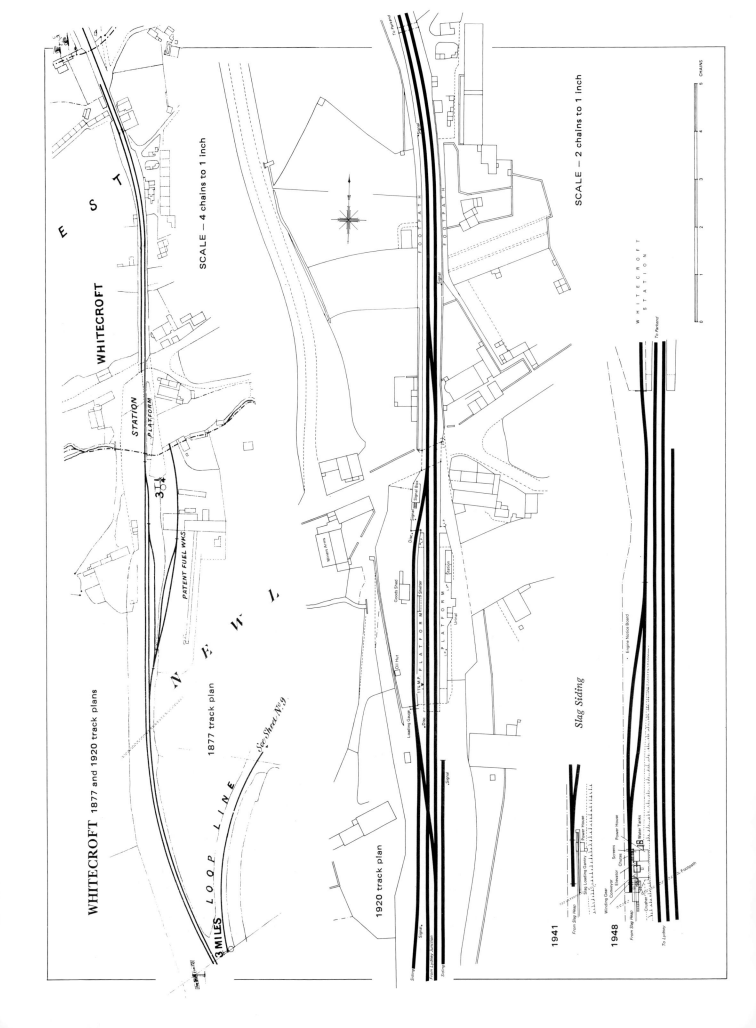

WHITECROFT 1877 and 1920 track plans

WHITECROFT

W E S T

N E W L

STATION

PLATFORM

3 MILES

LOOP LINE

PATENT FUEL WKS

See Sheet No.9

SCALE – 4 chains to 1 inch

1877 track plan

SCALE – 2 chains to 1 inch

To Parkend

FOOTPATH

FOOTPATH

Signal

Signal

Signal Box

Disc. Signal

Signal

Disc.

Signal Box

Goods Shed

Oil Hut

Shelter

P L A T F O R M

P L A T F O R M

Station

Urinal

1¾ M.P.

Loading Gauge

Disc.

Miner's Arms

Signal

From Lydney Junction

1920 track plan

CHAINS

0   1   2   3   4   5

Slag Siding

1941

From Slag Heap

Power House

Slag Loading Gantry

1948

Winding Gear

Elevator

Conveyor

Screens

Chutes

Power House

Crusher

From Slag Heap

Water Tanks

WHITECROFT STATION

To Parkend

Engine Notice Board

Footpath

To Lydney

A general view of Whitecroft with the Patent Fuel Works in the background.   *Collection N. Parkhouse*

line, evidently on the site later occupied by the second line of rails. This also provided access to cottages alongside the line and resulted in frequent trespass by the locals. In August 1877 the inhabitants were instructed not to use the course of the railway for carting dung as they had over the tramroad. A memorial had in fact been sent to the Home Office asking permission to use the railway for this purpose! However, in November the company's fears were realized when a man was killed near Whitecroft by a goods train, while he was trespassing in a state of intoxication. Another man was killed on the crossing on 6th October 1892 when

he was knocked down by a goods train. The gateman had ordered him to stand back but he persisted in crossing. The verdict was accidental death, with the recommendation that the footpath gates be interlocked with the signals. The decision to double the line clearly obliged the Joint Committee to do something about the rights of way. They proposed a footpath along either side of the line but the owners of the land required were unwilling to sell 'except at exorbitant prices'.

The company's solicitors were instructed to see whether the railway had the power to stop the trespassing, but their

Looking south through the station from the level crossing with the former Patent Fuel Works in the background and the sidings which served it. Eassie's original station building is the nearer half of the structure shown and the shortened platform at this end is particularly evident here.

Lens of Sutton

Whitecroft village and station c.1909.

Collection R. S. Carpenter

The signalman's view over the level crossing, probably c.1910. The lamp by the crossing was provided in 1907 to enable the signalman to satisfy himself that pedestrians were clear before locking the wicket gate. However, this did not prevent, in 1912, a trap driven by Police Superintendent Griffin of Coleford being caught in the gates and damaged. Superintendent Griffin was injured in this accident and received £10 in compensation from the Joint Committee. Needless to say, the hapless signalman was suitably cautioned! The upper sign behind the far crossing gate appears to be a Great Western and Midland Railway trespass notice whilst the lower 'Beware of Trains' notice is a standard Midland design with white letters on a blue background.

Collection N. Parkhouse

Looking north towards Parkend in 1933. The signal box, of which no photographs have been found, had been removed when the line was singled in 1930. It had formerly stood on the site of the tiny ground frame by the crossing. At this time the 'up' line on the right reverted to its former single line status whilst the 'down' line through the opposite platform remained only as a siding, the platform shelter having been removed in 1929 following the withdrawal of passenger services. The down inner home illustrated applied at this time to the single line. It was later replaced by the LMS tubular steel overhanging bracket shown on page 122.   *L. E. Copeland*

investigations proved otherwise and steps were taken to secure the necessary Parliamentary authorization for compulsory purchase of the land required.

The feeling of the local people who opposed the move is reflected in this letter from the Chairman of the West Dean Urban District Council to the Gaveller:

'I have personally been acquainted with it for more than a quarter of a century . . . . More than that I have walked with more than one funeral procession . . . . The joint company are attempting to practically abolish the right of way, or at any rate make it impractical for the people to use it as they have done hitherto. They have metalled the pathway preparatory to laying a second line of rails . . . . they refuse to open the gates which have been put up and so make it impossible for cottagers to carry goods to their houses or manure to their gardens. A funeral procession was subjected to a painful experience the other day by refusal of the railway official to open the gates in consequence of which they had to pass the coffin through the bars of the gate as best they could.'

A new road subsequently built between Whitecroft and Parkend effectively replaced the bridlepath, which the railway company later sought to close. This again raised at least some opposition, and a local newspaper in December 1902 described the new road as 'not a wide one and in dirty weather after much traffic it would be much more pleasant for foot passengers to use the bridle road.'

The new road was provided by the Crown and local authorities in order 'to attract more cyclists and tourists to

A closer view of the 1930 replacement ground frame supplied by the LMS, but a purely Midland design. It took over control of the existing up distant and home signals and down distant and inner home signals which thereafter applied to the single line, the up and down starting signals, up advanced starting signal and all ground discs being removed. It also controlled a new connection to the two sidings.   *R. Marrows*

WHITECROFT SIGNALLING DIAGRAMS 1897 and c.1930

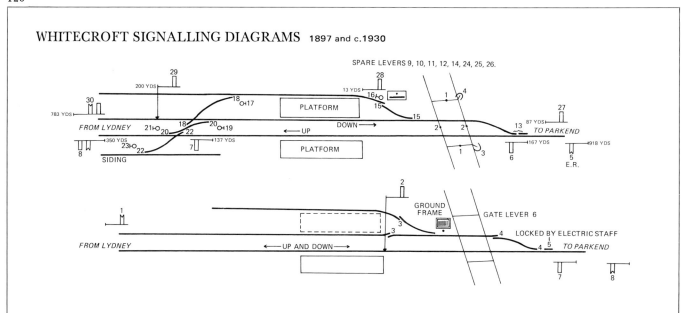

the area', and ultimately extended from Mierystock to Lydney when completed in 1904. It crossed the line at the existing level crossing and turned south east across the original station approach, being required by the Severn & Wye to keep to the level of the approach on either side.

The extinguishing of the committee's liability for the bridleway was provisionally agreed with the Crown in 1896, but it was not until 1905 that they were released upon payment of £100 to the Crown. The bridleway was truncated where it entered the woods just north of Whitecroft and a new path was provided to connect it from there to the new road.

In 1928 the station was staffed by a station master class 4, a clerk, a goods shunter class 2, two porters class 2, and two signalmen. The two signalmen at Tufts Junction and the gate woman at Pillowell Crossing on the Mineral Loop also came under Whitecroft for administrative purposes. After passenger closure in 1929 the following items of equipment were recorded for recovery:

Down Platform — open wood waiting shed, 1 fender, 1 lamp bracket, 1 stock ticket case, 2 ticket cases, 1 ticket dating press.
Platform equipment, etc. — 2 lamp standards (required for level crossing), 1 wheel barrow, 4 forms (platform), 6 lamps and standards.

The station master's office, booking & parcels office, and separate brick W.C. & urinal were retained whilst the booking hall and ladies W.C. were to be let. Other articles retained were 3 lamp standards (level crossing) and 1 two-wheel barrow.

WHITECROFT PATENT FUEL WORKS

The works were started in 1866-67 by the Compressed Coal Company to produce 'patent fuel' or briquettes from coal brought from the nearby Pillowell Level Colliery. The company applied to the Severn & Wye for permission to use the tramroad between Pillowell and Whitecroft. At the same time they were quoted a rate of 1/6d per ton for carriage of the finished article on the railway from Whitecroft to Lydney.

The manager of the new works was Mr. Lückes who, together with a Mr. Nash, were the galees of Pillowell Level. Lückes' proposal for a broad gauge branch to the Pillowell Level in 1868 was agreed by the Severn & Wye as long as

the Compressed Coal Company met the cost of building the branch. They were then reimbursed by means of reduced tolls, the agreed rebate being 6d per ton from Whitecroft to Lydney.

The works were evidently up for sale in 1877 as Severn & Wye minutes record that in March Messrs. Lückes and Nash were awaiting a buyer. It appears that by 1883 the works had passed to Simeon Holmes. He was the galee of Pillowell Level and it is highly probable that he already had an interest in the works. Certainly in 1889 Simeon Holmes' grandsons, Simeon Oaks Holmes and Peter Holmes, who traded as Holmes Bros., had set up the Forest of Dean Patent Fuel Company with Simeon Oaks Holmes as manager.

The concern soon changed hands again when the works were taken over by the Dean Forest Navigation Coal & Fuel Company. This was owned by Major Collins and Major Howell, and in 1893 it was reported to be one of the most prosperous concerns in the coalfield and also that the managing partner was Simeon Oaks Holmes. Prosperous or not, by 1896 the concern was in the hands of the Metropolitan Bank of Birmingham who were stated as being mortgagees.

In 1898 the various gales owned by the company, including Pillowell Level, Pillowell Engine or Random Shot,

A Dean Forest Navigation Coal & Fuel Company wagon.
Gloucester Railway Carriage & Wagon Co.

Yorkley, Bailey Hill, Howbeech and Blackpool Collieries, were put up for auction together with the fuel works and various cottages. The fuel works were described as being:

'held on a yearly tenancy at a rental of £120. The lease includes certain machinery and plant, a colliery office, house and garden, three enclosures of pasture land and four other cottages and gardens, in all about 15½ acres.

The above works are fitted with the latest machinery, the presses are Stevens patent and are capable of producing 100 tons of briquettes per day.

Machinery:- 2 Lancashire boilers, elevators, carriers, pitch crusher, disintegrator, two presses, shafting, railway siding, barrows, lathe, etc.

Also for sale 113 railway wagons (6, 8, 10 tons).'

It would appear that the sale did not go through, as the Metropolitan Bank informed the Crown in 1902 that they were desirous of surrendering the leases on the various gales. A trade directory of 1906 still mentions the Dean Forest Navigation Coal & Fuel Company with a Mr. William Richard as manager. In 1907 Pillowell Level and the other gales had been acquired by the Wallsend Colliery Company, who stated that they had no intention of working Pillowell Level. It is doubtful if they did any work at the fuel works either, as in 1910 the buildings were taken over by the Whitecroft Pin Manufacturing Company.

This firm was started by Maurice and Stanley Jarrett whose family were coal factors in the Forest. At first they employed six female workers, safety pins being the chief output. In 1947 the company became a subsidiary of the United Transport Company Limited, and in 1964 became part of the Scovill Manufacturing Company, an American concern. The works are still operating today under the name of Whitecroft-Scovill Limited.

The original siding into the works, which was connected to the long loop siding from Tufts Junction, divided into a loop and passed over a weighbridge before continuing on through the main building. At some stage after 1881, but before 1903, a second siding was added which also passed through the building.

These may have been taken out around 1910 when the fuel works closed, but they were certainly removed by 1922. The line from Tufts Junction remained as a long siding.

The gated southern entrance to the goods yard in April 1956, complete with standard timber framed GWR loading gauge. The offset approach to the slag siding can clearly be seen to the left, dating from the removal, in 1930, of the connection with the 'up' running line. *D. Thompson*

SLAG SIDING

A sizeable slag tip (about 50,000 tons) at the south of Whitecroft station belonged to the railway until 1931 when Arthur Morgan, managing director of Henry Crawshaw & Co., bought it for £250. Rail access was provided by extending the existing goods siding, for which he paid £30 per annum; a purpose built private siding and connections would have cost him some £900. The southernmost crossover to the yard had been removed with the singling and signal box closure in 1930, so, as it was then only connected to the single running line at the north end of the station, the whole siding had to be cleared in order to service Morgan's private extension.

Morgan appears to have formed a limited company in 1934, Arthur Morgan Ltd., but later in 1938 he sold out to

A closer view of Whitecroft station building on 17th July 1964. The original William Eassie structure is the further portion of this building, extending as far as the rainwater downpipe. The nearer section was added in October 1899 after a very unfavourable Board of Trade inspection and consisted of a waiting room, ladies room and ladies W.C. The half width structure at the 'Lydney' end is a later addition the purpose of which is unknown, but it may have been provided as a lamp hut when the signal box was removed. *A. K. Pope*

After the closure of Whitecroft signal box, the level crossing gates were hand operated. At some time during the final years, the double gates were replaced by the single ones shown here with their distinctive tall posts and ornate supporting brackets. The path from which this photograph was taken was provided to combat the trespassing discussed on page 115. *R. Marrows*

Roads Reconstruction (1934) Ltd. of Frome, Somerset. The new owners appear to have developed the site in 1941 by providing a slag loading gantry and power house together with a short passing loop between the goods yard and the end of the siding. This provided stabling for empty wagons which were then gravitated to the loading point as required, loaded wagons being drawn back to the adjacent line by a

powered capstan and wire rope. Each siding held approximately 6 or 7 wagons.

By 1948 the site had been taken over by Tytherington Stone Co. and a stone crushing plant was provided to replace the loading gantry, again in connection with the removal of slag, and was brought into use in December 1948. It is believed that a similar plant existed there before the last

Local traffic held while a coal train heads towards Lydney in the 1950s. The rear of the by now dilapidated ground frame shelter is visible to the right of the crossing gates. *A. K. Pope*

The entrance to the goods yard on 13th April 1967. Coal from smaller collieries was still being loaded at Whitecroft and Parkend around 1930. This was principally steam coal for the tinplate works etc. and was officially regarded as regular daily traffic. However, this scene, taken on 13th April 1967, shows a local coal merchant receiving supplies of house coal.
R. Marrows

war but this is not at all clear. Engines had not previously been allowed into either of the loop sidings, but the engine stop board was moved a short distance to the south to allow locomotives into the first few yards of each siding. The output appears to have increased from about three wagons a day to some four or five, but clearing the goods siding in order to service the private siding was not popular with the staff and caused delays at the level crossing. Three roads converged adjacent to the crossing, which was consequently busy; it was also crossed by four bus routes. The station master suggested an additional but more direct connection to the siding from the former 'down' line, then used for wagon storage, but as this would have cost about £1,000 it was not conceded. The clearing of the slag heap took several years.

A Lydney bound train passing the Whitecroft distant signal in June 1964. The black and white bands were a style of painting adopted by the LMS to ease the sighting of such signals at a distance.
R. Marrows

124

A superb view of the station taken in the early years of this century. The extensions on either end of the original Eassie station building are clearly distinguishable by the different tones of roof slates. The ruins of Parkend ironworks are visible behind the station building.

A postcard view of Parkend c.1910 showing the 'up' platform shelter on the extreme right. In contrast to the previous view, the ironworks chimney has been demolished and the corrugated hut in front of the goods shed has been removed, whilst the signals have been repainted in Midland style.

Lens of Sutton

PARKEND

The village of Parkend was an important industrial centre well served by tramroads from an early date. There were iron furnaces and a tinplate works within the village, stone quarries to the west, two stone works and many surrounding coal mining concerns. However, as will be seen, the arrival of the railway coincided with a decline in the industrial fortunes of the village.

When the railway reached Parkend in 1868 it was as a single line of broad gauge alongside the tramroad. A siding was also laid to the ironworks that year. It soon became necessary to provide accommodation for local trade and in 1869 a siding was laid alongside the Milkwall branch tramroad to an area known as 'the Marsh', where a new loading wharf was built. It was served by a siding on either side, the outer of two more to the south serving a goods shed built in 1871 by Messrs. Eassie & Co. In 1875 extra land was leased from the Crown to enable a headshunt to be added to the southern sidings. It was also proposed at about this time to extend the line serving the Marsh to join the Coleford branch then under construction, but nothing came of this.

By 1873 another siding belonging to the ironworks had been laid alongside the goods branch and terminated at a wharf, just short of the Fountain Inn, which probably had some connection with the nearby cinder tips. On 1877 Severn & Wye plans, two more short sidings are also shown going into the cinder tips, again from what became known

as the 'goods branch' or 'Parkend goods', but curving back to the south.

The tramroad alongside the goods branch remained until after the closure of the ironworks in 1877, when it was terminated on the loading wharf, and the redundant section subsequently removed. The Milkwall branch tramroad was abandoned after 1876, but the lower portion was retained to link the privately owned Oakwood Tramroad to Parkend wharf and continued in use until around 1914.

The passenger station not only served Parkend but was also the junction station for the Coleford branch. It was equipped with a crossing loop, two platforms, one of Eassie's station buildings, separate timber urinals similar to those at Whitecroft, and a footbridge. The platforms had been constructed by 1873, some excavation, on land purchased from the owners of Parkend House, being necessary for the 'up' platform which was backed by a substantial retaining wall. By 1877 a loop siding is shown behind the 'down' platform.

The 1896 doubling between Whitecroft and Parkend brought the inevitable Board of Trade inspection and, as with Whitecroft, the inspecting officer was not impressed with the accommodation. He gave six months to put it into a reasonable state. A new signal box was also provided at this time to replace the original box or lever frame (of which no details have so far been discovered), formerly situated at the Lydney end of the 'up' platform. In the event it was not until July 1898 that the Severn & Wye engineer prepared the plans for the required improvements to the station accommodation, and not until January 1900

Looking towards the station c.1910-15 with the remains of the siding into the ironworks cinder tips on the left. The siding comes off a headshunt for the goods branch.

Collection E. Gwynne

that the alterations, costing some £260, were completed and approved by the Board of Trade, almost four years after their six months deadline.

In 1897 the goods shed from the Marsh was moved to the station and positioned by the siding behind the 'down' platform. The move, estimated at £75 which included £20 for refurbishment of the structure, was carried out because of its inconvenient situation some 500 yards from the station, where it was apparently of little use for storage purposes as it was infested with vermin from an adjacent stream.

In July 1898 an application for a temporary siding was made by Cruwys & Hobrough, a firm of contractors from Gloucester. This enabled them to remove about 10,000 tons of slag and cinders from the ironworks tips (started in 1836) for use as ballast in Gloucester. The siding cost £60 for labour and £20 per annum for the hire of permanent way materials.

Early in 1899 the Commissioners of Woods wrote to the railway asking whether the siding could be left *in situ* for a couple of years after the contractors had finished using it. They wanted slag for use in the construction of the new road being planned through the Forest from Mierystock to Lydney. However, the Severn & Wye were not particularly co-operative and required an undertaking that at least 1,500 to 2,000 tons of slag would be loaded at the siding, realizing some £150-£200.

The Commissioners pointed out that this worked out at 2/- per ton for the five miles to Speech House Road station.

The Crown Deputy Surveyor then pointed out that the Severn & Wye had laid the siding on Crown land without permission and that, unless it was left *in situ* in case they wished to use it, they would either have them remove it immediately or charge for the tonnage of material taken over it. The outcome is not clear, but it was out of use by January 1900 and removed by 1902/4 when the new road was eventually built through Parkend.

The staff establishment at Parkend seems to have remained fairly stable, the complement of eleven in 1904 changing to ten in 1928 when there was a stationmaster, a clerk, two signalmen class 5, and two porters class 2, together with two signalmen class 5 for Travellers Rest and two signalmen class 4 for Coleford Junction.

When the station closed to passengers in 1929 the following items were recovered:

Down Platform — wooden station building.
Up Platform — open wood waiting shed.
Platform equipment etc. — 5 wall lamps, 5 forms, 2 one-wheel barrows, 3 fire buckets and brackets, 1 Nestlés sweet machine (to be returned to owners), 1 cupboard, 1 ticket dating press, 2 ticket cases, 1 stock ticket case, 1 weighing machine 2 cwts., 4 bracket lamps in office and waiting rooms, 1 stove in office, 3 fenders.

The brick urinal and W.C. on the 'down' platform were to be retained along with the following: 5 lamp standards, 1 two-wheel barrow, 1 four-wheel trolley, 1 sack truck, 2 lamp standards (level crossing) and 1 parcels sheet LM & S.

Looking towards the station from the top of the cinder tips. A passenger train composed of GWR 4 and 6 wheeled coaches can be seen in the platform. The fence in the right foreground is part of that around the station master's house. *Lens of Sutton*

The Cross, Parkend, with the goods branch in the foreground. The road crossing it is part of the one constructed by the Crown around 1902-4 to provide a new access into the Forest. The old ironworks engine house, now converted into a Forestry school, is also featured.

Collection N. Parkhouse

Looking back towards Whitecroft from the footbridge in September 1946 with the remains of the 'down' line terminating at the buffer stop and the headshunt from the goods branch petering out into the undergrowth. The up starting and down home signals and the down main to siding bracket signal shared the same post from the time of the 1930 singling.

L. E. Copeland

The goods branch curving off to the left past the station master's house.

Collection R. S. Carpenter

GWR '57XX' class 0—6—0PT No. 4698 on the goods branch on 6th August 1965. *W. Potter*

The Fountain Inn with the goods branch on the left. In 1900 this stretch of line was unfenced, which led to a gentleman writing to the Commissioners of Woods pointing out that it was bad enough stepping out of the Inn onto a public road but that, if this were successfully negotiated, he was onto an unfenced railway where shunting was often taking place at night! *Collection N. Parkhouse*

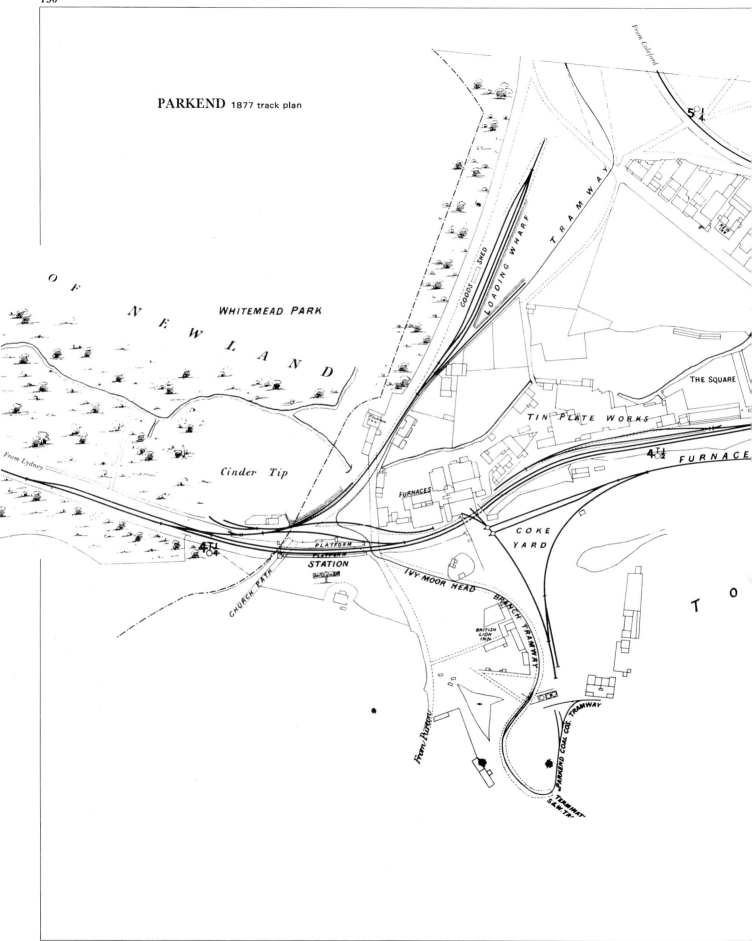

PARKEND 1877 track plan

OF NEWLAND

WHITEMEAD PARK

From Coleford

5 ¼

GOODS SHED

LOADING WHARF

TRAMWAY

THE SQUARE

TIN PLATE WORKS

From Lydney

Cinder Tip

FURNACES

4 T ½

FURNACE

COKE YARD

4 T 4

CHURCH PATH

PLATFORM

STATION

PLATFORM

IVY MOOR HEAD

T O

From Purton

BRITISH LION INN

BRANCH TRAMWAY

PARKEND COAL CO? TRAMWAY

TERMINAT SAW TR

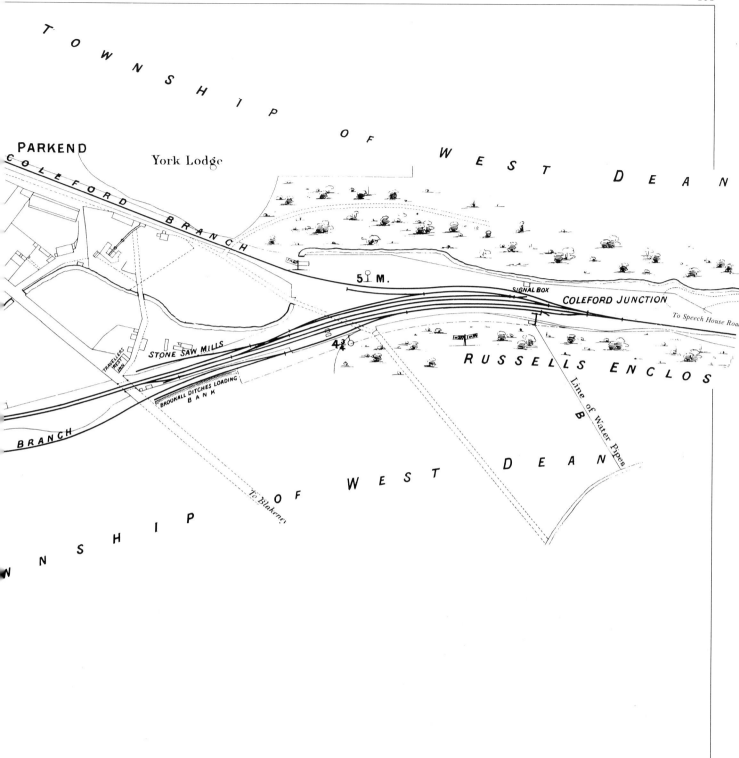

PARKEND

York Lodge

T O W N S H I P   O F   W E S T   D E A N

COLEFORD BRANCH

5 M.

SIGNAL BOX

COLEFORD JUNCTION

To Speech House Road

STONE SAW MILLS

TRAVELLERS REST INN

4½

BROOKALL DITCHES LOADING BANK

R U S S E L L S   E N C L O S

B

Line of Water Pipes

BRANCH

To Blakeney

N S H I P   O F   W E S T   D E A N

W

S c a l e .

100 50 0   1   2   3   4   5   6   7   8   9   10 Chains

PARKEND 1898 and 1920 track plans

1898 track plan

Loading Wharves

Crane

To Coleford

13¼

Chapel

Steam Saw Mills

New Inn

The Square

12½

Cannop Brook

Fountain Inn

Cinder Tip

12¼

Parkend Iron Furnaces
(Dismantled)

PARKEND ROYAL BRANCH

From Lydney

Signal

Pipes leading from Well

TANK

Goods Shed

Signal Box

Signal

Signal

Signal

Signal

DISC

PLATFORM

PLATFORM

Pond

The British Lion

Joint Railway Co.
maintain to this point

A   A

C I N D E R   T I P

From Lydney Junction

Bridle Path

Signal

Station Master's House

Goods Shed

12½ M.P.

Oil

Coal

Urinal

PLATFORM

PLATFORM

Church Path

1920 track plan

SCALE — 2 chains to 1 inch

0   1   2   3   4   5   CHAINS

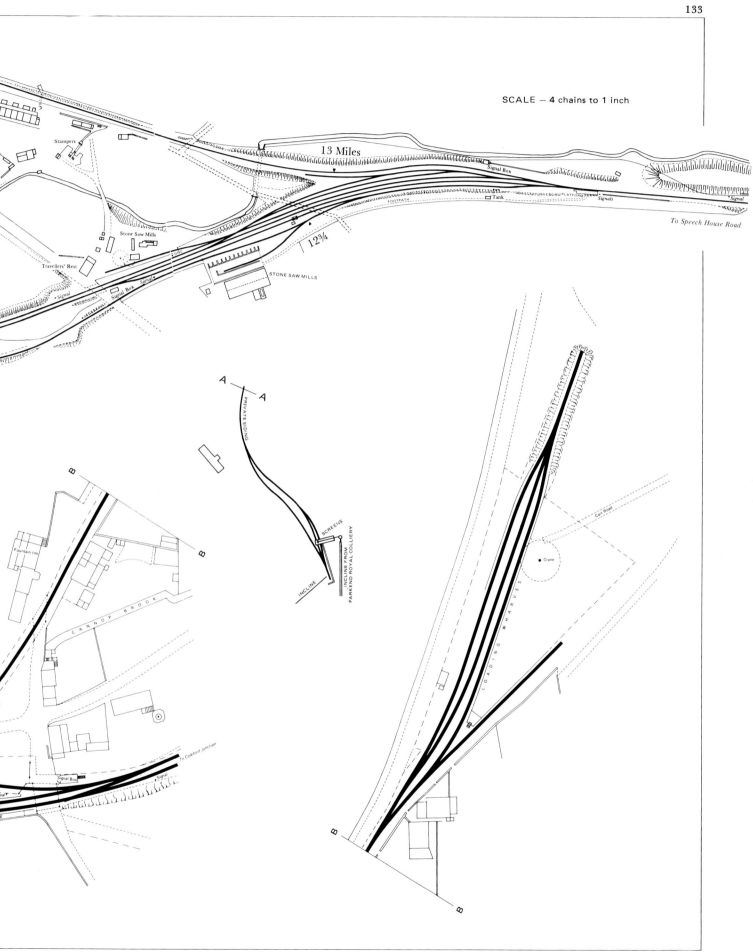

SCALE — 4 chains to 1 inch

13 Miles

Signal Box

Stampers

Stone Saw Mills

Travellers' Rest

Signal Box   Signal

STONE SAW MILLS

12¾

Tank   PLATFORM   Signals

FOOTPATH   Signal

To Speech House Road

A   A

PRIVATE SIDING

SCREENS

INCLINE FROM PARKEND ROYAL COLLIERY

INCLINE

B   B

Fountain Inn

CANNOP BROOK

To Coleford Junction

Signal Box   Signal

B   B

LOADING WHARVES

Crane

Cart Road

B   B

134

Looking into the Marsh sidings on 21st September 1947. The Milkwall branch tramroad came down the track on the right, whilst the Oakwood Tramroad later terminated in a series of sidings on top of the loading wharf in the centre. The Marsh sidings were laid on a slight rising gradient, and in 1921 a rake of six loaded wagons ran away and damaged the crossing gates opposite the Fountain Inn. As a result, the wheel scotches seen at the entrance to each siding were provided in 1922 at a cost of £18.

L. E. Copeland

Parkend Goods in the 1930s. The original site of the goods shed was approximately where the tree trunks are lying alongside the road. The Castlemain pumping engine of Parkend Colliery can also be seen on the hillside in the background. *Collection A. K. Pope*

Looking down into Marsh sidings from above the headshunt in September 1946. *L. E. Copeland*

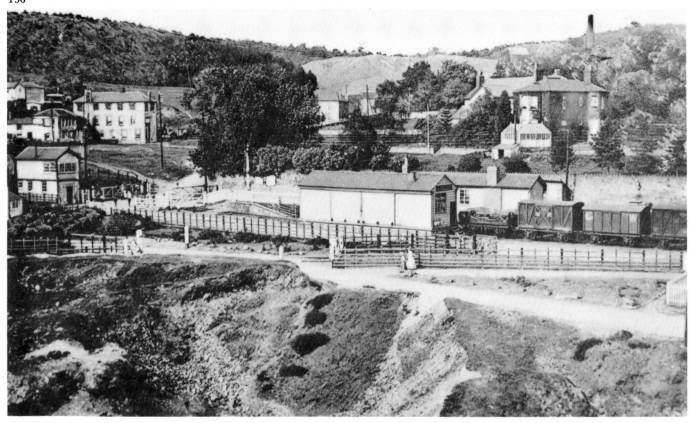

A similar view to that on page 127 but showing more detail in the station area. The large dwelling above the station buildings is Parkend House and to the left, above the signal box, the British Lion public house can be seen. *Collection N. Parkhouse*

A Lydney bound train consisting of three GWR 4-wheel brake 3rds with a Midland milk van nearest the engine, at Parkend in the early 1920s. Standard Midland Railway lamps and one of the company's rustic station seats are in evidence. *H. J. Patterson Rutherford*

Another view of the station from the footbridge in 1933. Although only four years after the cessation of passenger traffic, all buildings and platform fittings, except for the brick built urinal, have been removed. Had the proposal, in September 1932, to restore passenger services between Lydney Town and Parkend on Saturdays been carried through, the platform lighting would have been restored and a portable building provided to serve as a booking office.   *L. E. Copeland*

The footbridge was provided to enable passengers to cross the line as Parkend was the junction station for Coleford and connections were made here. It also maintained access to a footpath running to Parkend church. The date that a footbridge was first provided is unknown, the one illustrated being an 1899 replacement. The original was slightly further towards Coleford Junction and it would appear from drawings that the replacement was virtually built around it. The contract for the new bridge was awarded in May 1899 to Finch & Co. Ltd. of Chepstow who provided it for the sum of £464 7s. 4d.

The water column on the end of the 'up' platform was standard Great Western equipment although the date of its provision has not been discovered. From August 1888 the Midland were charged 4d each time their locos took water here, but a Lydney driver recalls that, later at least, water was not often taken here as it appears that the supply was variable. A local stream, via pipes, fed a small tank in the woods above the column, but this was often blocked by leaves. The Severn & Wye paid the Crown £1 per annum for leave to use the water for locomotives, but in 1899 were caught by the Crown's Deputy Surveyor making a connection to take water to the urinal from the water column supply, which he doubted they had permission to do under the original licence!

J. Dagley-Morris

A postcard view of the Cross, looking up the road to Yorkley. The original was postmarked 1914.   *Collection A. K. Pope*

Looking north over the level crossing on 5th June 1933. The gates in the platform fence serve what appears to be a small loading wharf visible to the left of the goods shed in the view on page 136.
                                                                                                          L. E. Copeland

Parkend signal box and level crossing looking south in January 1961. The gate over the northern end of the goods loop can be seen on the far side of the road behind the main crossing gate.

R. Dagley-Morris

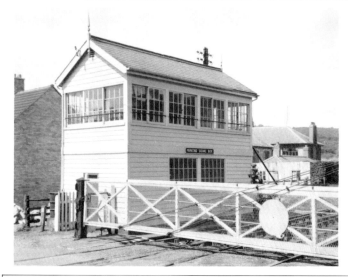

Whilst contemporary with and sharing the same style as those at Lydney Town, Tufts Junction, Whitecroft and Travellers Rest, Parkend signal box was constructed of timber. Again it was situated alongside the level crossing and housed a gate wheel for operating the gates. As with Whitecroft, during the final years the double gates featured in other views were replaced with the long single span ones illustrated here, the gate wheel being superseded by simple hand operation. The taller gate posts were necessary for the bracing rods supporting the extra weight of the long frames.

A. K. Pope

PARKEND SIGNAL BOX DIAGRAMS 1897 and c.1930

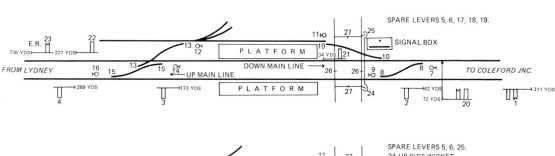

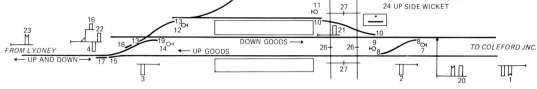

Dean Goods 0—6—0 No. 2515 at Parkend on 21st September 1947 with a permanent way train.   *L. E. Copeland*

Relaying the 'up' line just north of the level crossing in 1947. The train in the preceding view was run in conjunction with this work.

L. E. Copeland

Looking north through the curves between Parkend and Travellers Rest. The end of the fence on the left would be approximately where a siding went into the iron-works in 1873. The sloping wall on the right is the remains of the 'covered way' removed in 1898.

M. Rees

PARKEND IRON FURNACES

Situated just north of the level crossing on the 'down' side of the line, the ironworks were served by the siding already mentioned as extant by 1869. This siding, however, may have been removed in 1873 in connection with the construction of the station. It is likely that to maintain a rail outlet for the works another siding was laid into the works trailing off the 'down' main beyond the level crossing. This is shown on a plan of 1873, but it had been removed by 1877 when once again a siding was laid off the goods branch. This latter siding was undoubtedly owned by the ironworks company but its exact date of removal is unknown. It was still *in situ* in 1903 and may have been used for loading crushed slag, again by Messrs. Cruwys & Hobrough.

A single blasting furnace stood on the site in 1799, with bellows operated by a steam engine. By 1807 the concern was owned by a Mr. Perkins, but, due to inefficient smelting of Forest iron by coke, the works fell idle at about this time. They were purchased by John Protheroe, a local colliery owner, who in turn sold them in 1824 to his nephew Edward Protheroe, owner of extensive coal mines in the Parkend area. He leased the works for 42 years to the Forest of Dean Iron Company formed by Moses Teague, William Montague and Benjamin Whitehouse.

In 1825 the company made a reservoir for the works further up the valley of the Cannop Brook. They utilised the embankment of the Severn & Wye Bicslade branch for the dam, thus forming the lower Cannop Pond, and the water from this was led to the works along a leat to a pond east of the furnace. By late 1826 there were complaints that the dam had lowered the water level in the canal at Lydney, by interfering with the natural flow of the Cannop Brook which fed it.

By 1826 the lessees of the works were William Montague and John James who, in 1827, erected a 51 feet diameter waterwheel to create the blast for the furnace. However, even though extra water supplies were tapped, the wheel was not a success and by May 1827 the company decided they had no alternative but to revert to steam power. The Crown's deputy surveyor insisted that a tall chimney stack for the new 90 horse power engine should be built of such a height that the smoke would be 'dissipated and rendered less injurious', (he lived virtually next door!). The steam engine did not prove a success either and so a second pond was added at Cannop to boost the supply of water to the wheel.

It was the practice in the eighteenth century to build iron furnaces close to a hillside to enable the coke, limestone and iron-ore to be transported via a bridge to the top of the furnace for charging. A structure such as this certainly existed to serve the original furnaces at Parkend, but it is not known whether the main line of tramroad passed under this when it was laid in 1810/12, or if the bridge had been removed. During the rebuilding of the furnaces in 1825 a new bridge was built, forming an artificial tunnel over the tramroad. Tramroads and the water supply to the wheel ran across it whilst built into the structure were eight cottages! This structure and the space beneath was known as the 'covered-way'. During the 1850s when the Severn & Wye was debating converting the tramroad to a broad gauge railway, a contract was drawn up for rebuilding the covered-way. This, however, was not done until 1870 when the Iron Company required a larger bridge to serve a third furnace then under construction, a second having been added in 1827.

A large area on the hillside opposite the ironworks had been leased from the Office of Woods in 1829 to form what was known as the coke yard, and it was here that materials for the furnace were collected together and stored. A survey of 1835 shows that, in addition to two furnaces and the covered-way, the works consisted of a coke hearth, casting house, engine houses, boilers, carpenter's and blacksmith's shops, stables, a counting house, workshops and offices, together with a beer house, a house for the agent, four 'good houses for workmen' and the eight cottages built into the covered-way.

In 1836 the company leased an acre of land to the south of the works, between the Cannop Brook and the tramroad, from the Office of Woods for the purpose of tipping cinders from the furnace. In 1850 a further acre was leased to increase the tipping space and, as already mentioned, the removal of 'the cinder tip' was under way in 1899.

Business fluctuated between 1829 and 1841; by February 1841 output had risen to 100 tons of pig iron a week, but by the Autumn the works were idle. They re-opened in 1846 and, following Montague's death in 1847, James became the sole lessee. In 1854 he bought the freehold from Protheroe and placed the works under the management of Charles Greenham, who became a partner. The

Parkend iron furnaces c.1880. The building on the right housed the blowing engine used to create the 'blast' or draught within the furnaces. The two earlier furnaces are housed in the stone building on the left and to their right can be seen the steel cased furnace added in the early 1870s.

Collection A. K. Pope

firm continued to trade as the Forest of Dean Iron Company, adding iron forges and rolling mills to the works and also building a tinplate works nearby. In 1846 about 280 tons of pig iron were being produced a week.

The business boomed, and when the third furnace was built in 1871 all three were in blast, the iron mainly being used in the production of steel plates and tinplate. James again became sole owner when Greenham died in 1866.

In 1875, following a depression in the trade, Edwin Crawshay purchased the ironworks and the adjacent tinplate works. He hoped that they would continue to show a profit, but they were soon taken over by Henry Crawshay & Company who owned many other iron and coal concerns within the Forest. The depression continued and during 1877 only one furnace was in blast, and by the end of the year the works were closed. Despite many rumours of takeovers and re-opening, they remained silent until 1890, when demolition started. The covered-way was removed in 1898, and the large stack was felled in 1908 when the engine house was converted to a Forestry school. By 1892 ownership of the land had passed to Mr. T. H. Deakin, the owner of Parkend Deep Navigation Collieries Ltd.

A broad gauge branch to serve the ironworks was built c.1869. It left the main line at what later became Coleford Junction and ran behind the later site of Travellers Rest signal box, where it crossed the Parkend-Blakeney road. Beyond this point the track was owned by the ironworks company and was known as the Furnace branch. It was 26 chains in length and terminated in the coke yards. In 1873 Brookhall Ditches siding was laid on the site later occupied by David & Company's stone works to the north of Travellers Rest. The siding was built to enable coal to be taken from the Brookhall Ditches pits of the Parkend Coal Company up the Furnace branch to the coke yard. Wagons

coming off the siding passed over about 50 yards of Severn & Wye track and a toll of 2d per ton was charged for this privilege, plus 6d per ton for hauling the loaded trucks up the Iron Company's branch.

The Furnace branch was out of use from 1877, when the ironworks closed, until the Parkend Colliery was re-opened in 1887, when the Severn & Wye paid the Crawshays a wayleave for traffic over the line. In 1891 the branch was sold to the colliery concern.

PARKEND TINPLATE WORKS

The tinplate works adjoined the ironworks and lay between the Cannop Brook and the tramroad, being served by a siding on the 'down' side, which divided into a loop once inside the works boundary. The complex included iron forges and rolling mills built between 1851 and 1853 by John James and Charles Greenham who, as already mentioned, were lessees of the Parkend ironworks. Once construction of the works was under way, James and Greenham took out a 31 year lease on Crown land just north of the site, where they built twenty-four houses for their workers.

James and Greenham did not keep the works long after they had completed them. By the autumn of 1854 the owner was Samuel Ries who in turn leased them to Nathaniel Daniels, who was trading as the Parkend Plate Company. Daniels, however, was not very successful. He was insolvent by December 1854 and a trustee was appointed to sell the assets. In 1856 the works were bought by the Allaways of Lydney tinplate works and by 1866 two hundred people were employed there producing about five hundred boxes of tinplate a week.

In 1872 the works were put up for auction, notices advertising the sale stating that they comprised about seven acres of freehold land, the fixed plant, machinery and

A general view of Parkend.
Collection N. Parkhouse

Two views of the dwellings built for the workers at the tinplate works in 1851. They were three storeys high and had six rooms each and, laid out in two blocks of twelve at right angles to each other, became known locally as 'The Square'.

Mrs. D. Pope and E. Parker

The houses in this view were built on the ironworks site and fronted onto the Parkend-Lydbrook road, part of the 'new road' built by the Crown. Above them can be seen a shunt signal on the Parkend Royal branch which served the Parkend Colliery seen in the background. This may have been provided in 1904 when it was thought desirable to have a signal to regulate trains from the colliery.

Collection E. Gwynne

rolling stock. Also included were a house for the proprietor, a manager's house, storehouse, warehouses, offices, carpenter's and blacksmith's shops, stables and the twenty-four workers houses.

In 1875 Edwin Crawshay bought the works at the same time that he purchased the ironworks, and the following year was producing 700 to 800 boxes of tinplate a week. The slump of 1875 to 1878, however, meant that the Crawshays' prosperity was short-lived. The fortunes of the tinworks were no doubt closely linked to those of the ironworks and both passed to Henry Crawshay and Son in January 1877, ceasing production in August. In 1879 the tinworks were leased to Charles Morris of Llanelly for a period of 14 years. Workmen began to renovate the machinery and in 1880 both mills were working again, but in August 1881 Morris gave a month's notice to his workers. Two hundred were made redundant on 21st September and the works remained closed until 1900, when they were demolished. The square remained until the houses, in a very dilapidated state, were demolished in the mid 1950s.

PARKEND COLLIERY

In the 1841 coal awards, nine colliery concerns were defined in the Parkend area. Of these Edward Protheroe had an interest in five including the largest — Parkend Colliery. The others were Venus & Jupiter, Catch Can, Independent Level and New Fancy. When Protheroe died in 1857 he still owned Parkend and New Fancy which were sold by his

One of the Royal shafts of Parkend Colliery c.1912. This was the main coal raising shaft and loaded tubs were let down an incline from here to the screens near the Castlemain shaft.

Collection A. K. Pope

Parkend Castlemain. The building on the right housed a 78 inch diameter cylinder beam engine used for pumping water from Parkend Colliery and later New Fancy Colliery.   *Collection A. K. Pope*

executors to Messrs. James W. Sully, T. Sully, J. Trotter and T. Nicholson, who traded under the name of the Parkend Coal Company. They already owned Standfast and Royal Engine Pit, Catch Can and Independent Level collieries, and the acquisition of Parkend and New Fancy meant that they now owned virtually all the collieries in the Parkend area.

In December 1878 James Sully was the only partner left and a new limited company, the Parkend Coal Co. Ltd., was formed to take over the collieries from him. The capital was £80,000 in one thousand £80 shares, Sully owning 967 of them. The new company did not prosper and in March 1880, following a slump in the coal trade, the pits closed, throwing 700 men and boys out of employment, and in April the company went into voluntary liquidation.

In May 1881 the collieries were put up for auction, Standfast and Royal Engine, Independent Level and Catch Can were described as being of minor importance but desirable for the protection of the Parkend and New Fancy gales. The total area of this group was 1,240 acres, of which Parkend and New Fancy formed 1,150. The output in 1879 was stated as being 101,198 tons with an estimated workable reserve of eleven million tons. Parkend colliery had one pumping pit (Castlemain), which was 150 yards deep, and two other pits (Parkend Royal), one being 199 yards deep and the other 140 yards. Included in the sale were the engine houses, pit machinery, sidings, trams, horses and an enclosed yard at Parkend with stabling for twenty horses, a coach house loft, fitter's, smith's and blacksmith's shops, a weigh house and lodges, sheds, stores and offices. There were also thirty stone built workmen's cottages at Whitecroft, two at Standfast, two at Brookhall Ditches and one at Moseley Green, all of which had gardens. There was a bailiff's house at New Fancy and an excellent manager's house at Parkend, known as Parkend House, with stables, outbuildings, a garden and a paddock of about one acre in area.

This view of Castlemain c.1902 shows the end of the beam projecting through the 'bob wall' of the engine house. The shaft was 450 feet deep and the water was raised in 3 lifts up a pipe, the 'rising main'. The engine had a 9 foot stroke and worked at 8½ strokes per minute lifting 700 gallons of water in that time. The lightweight headframe was used to remove the pump rod, seen here hanging from the beam, for repair if necessary.   *Collection A. K. Pope*

Parkend Colliery, possibly about 1900. The primitive nature of the screens can be seen and also, to the left, the incline which brought the tubs of coal from the Royal shafts. Behind the screens another incline can be discerned as shown on the 1898 plan on page 132. This incline was probably used to supply coal to the boilers at Castlemain. Notice also the smaller Cornish beam engine to the left of the main pumping house. *Collection A. K. Pope*

A pair of Parkend Deep Navigation Collieries Ltd. wagons.
Gloucester Railway Carriage & Wagon Co. and L. E. Copeland

The collieries were bought by a Mr. Jackson who appointed Thomas Hedges Deakin as manager. Deakin had been born in Pontypool in 1850 and began working in a colliery at the age of 13½. In 1877 he had been appointed manager of Trafalgar Colliery, at Brierley, which was one of the largest in the Forest. He was a Methodist lay preacher, a non-smoker and teetotaller and took up residence in Parkend House. Under his management, the collieries prospered, but in 1883 they were forced to close due to financial difficulties, apparently being heavily mortgaged. The following year they were bought by Deakin and two partners in an auction at Gloucester.

By April 1885 the collieries were owned by Deakin and a Mrs. Susan Broadley. The Parkend & New Fancy Collieries Company was set up to purchase the collieries from them, the first directors being Deakin, Mrs. Broadley and Frank Step Hockaday. Deakin, as chairman, managing director and mining agent, appointed William Cooper as manager and throughout the 1880s the collieries prospered, producing on average 80,000 tons per year.

The workings of Parkend and New Fancy Collieries were by now clearly interwoven, as in January 1888 the company wrote to the Crown asking for a reduction in the wayleaves paid. It would appear that for the purposes of working the two gales more economically some Parkend coal was being brought to the surface up the New Fancy shaft. Its proximity to the area being worked by Parkend enabled haulage costs to be reduced, but because the coal was passed through the Parkend barrier into an adjoining area, a wayleave of 1d per ton was charged. The company pleaded that it was working inferior coal to its predecessors, and, since more water was having to be pumped out of the pit, the wayleave was crippling them. The Crown saw reason in this and, doubtless not wanting the pit to close (they would lose the income from the rent), relented and reduced the wayleave on 30th June 1888 to ½d per ton.

Looking towards Travellers Rest level crossing on 22nd June 1947. The route of the Parkend Royal branch can be made out running between the low bank and the hillside.   *L. E. Copeland*

The company was wound up voluntarily in March 1892 and replaced by the Parkend Deep Navigation Company Limited. Deakin remained as managing director until he died in 1935 at the age of 85, his son succeeding him and continuing in office until 1942.

Parkend Colliery ceased to produce coal in 1929, but Parkend Royal pit remained connected underground to New Fancy to provide an emergency exit, Castlemain shaft

also being kept open to pump water and provide air for New Fancy until that colliery's closure in 1944. In February 1944 an advertisement was placed in local papers advising of the surrender of the gales and asking for applicants to take them over, but there were no offers and the pits closed.

The railway connection to Parkend Colliery was made in 1887 by extending the Furnace branch belonging to the

A view on the same date as that above and looking back towards Parkend with Travellers Rest signal box on the left. The two wagons are standing on the remains of the colliery branch which continued in use as a siding north of the road.   *L. E. Copeland*

TRAVELLERS REST SIGNAL BOX DIAGRAM c.1911

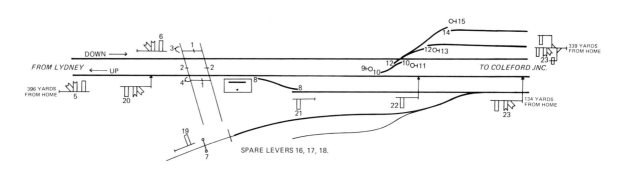

ironworks. It came to be known as the Parkend Royal branch and was taken over by the colliery company. In 1891 the Severn & Wye became responsible for its upkeep, as far as a point alongside the British Lion Public House and in 1894 it was taken over by the Joint Committee. Beyond this the line remained the responsibility of the colliery company. It was laid on land leased from the Crown and this section of track led to a few disputes between the company and the Crown, the most notable being in 1902. In April of that year the colliery company wanted to lengthen its full wagon road, as it was not long enough to hold a train without running foul of the points of the empty wagon road, and wrote to the Crown stating their intentions and asking permission for the work to proceed.

There had, however, been a complaint to the Crown in 1900 about the lack of level crossing gates on the Parkend Royal Branch at Travellers Rest. The colliery company were liable for the cost of installing these gates and, as nothing had been done about them, the Crown refused permission for the extension of the siding until they had been provided. The dispute continued for several months with neither side giving way, until pressure of traffic forced the colliery company to provide the crossing gates.

Special regulations applied to the working of the branch and the following is an extract from the Appendix of 1911:-

Before a train is allowed to leave Coleford Junction Yard for Parkend Royal Colliery, the Signalman at Travellers' Rest must

A close-up of Travellers Rest box, a standard GWR design, probably built in 1897 when the intermediate post here was made a block post, and worked by a signalman and porter-signalman instead of the two porter-signalmen previously employed. *Collection A. K. Pope*

A postcard view of a local shop and village hall. It was taken looking down the Coleford-Blakeney road through Parkend and just shows Travellers Rest crossing in the middle distance.

Collection R. How

Looking down the same road, but in the opposite direction to the previous view. The gate on the right formerly closed across the Parkend Royal branch. The Railway Inn on the far side of the crossing was earlier known as the 'Travellers' Rest' and before that 'The Bear'. It closed in 1959.

A. K. Pope

The crossing on 7th June 1960. Again the single span gates here replaced shorter double ones during the final years, the originals being worked from a gate wheel in the box, the replacements by hand. *A. K. Pope*

satisfy himself that the crossing is clear, and the gates properly secured across the Highway Road, and before the train starts must in like manner satisfy himself that the Branch is clear. The train must then proceed up the gradient cautiously, and either the Guard or the Brakesman must walk in front of the wagons that are being propelled.

The Outwards traffic from the Colliery will be picked up from the Outwards Siding, and when the train is ready to leave, the Engine-driver must give one short whistle and one crow, and the signalman in charge of the Travellers' Rest signal box will then ask the signalman at Coleford Junction on the Telephone or Single Needle Instrument if the Line is clear for the train to

leave the Colliery Siding, and after the signalman at Coleford Junction has given the necessary permission he must not allow any train to foul the running line until the train from the Colliery Siding has come to a stand in the Coleford Junction Yard. All messages sent to be entered in the train register book.

The signalman at the Travellers' Rest Signal Box having obtained 'Line Clear' from the signalman at Coleford Junction must close the Level Crossing Gates and properly fasten them against the Highway, and then lower the starting signal for the train to leave the Colliery Siding.

Drivers must be particularly careful and not allow their engines to pass over the catch points from the Colliery Siding in the direction of Coleford Junction until the starting signal has been lowered, and they must stop opposite the weighbridge clear of the crossing of No. 3 siding, Coleford Junction, for the purpose of adjusting wagon brakes.

PARKEND STONEWORKS

Stone had been quarried in Dean before 450 BC, and by 1858 there were about 360 operative quarries in the area. These were mainly working 'Forest Blue Stone' which is a sandstone from the coal measures. This occurs in shades of blue and grey and commanded a high price as monumental and better class building stone.

Parkend was a centre for stone works, the first being established here in 1850. In 1870 E. R. Payne set up a stone saw mills just off the Parkend-Blakeney road, behind the Travellers Rest Inn. The works were served by a siding connected to the 'down' main line and provided in 1889 at Payne's expense. A travelling crane was also installed at the same time. Stone was brought in from the company's quarries at Bicslade, just south of Speech House Road, and Point Quarry, alongside the Coleford branch, which also had its own siding and saw mills. In 1910 the company was acquired by the United Stone Firms Company Limited, who apparently did not look too closely at what they were

Signalman Ferd Wilkins in Travellers Rest box on 24th April 1967. For many years his brother Fred was signalman at Parkend. The double line block instruments on the block shelf are of Midland Railway pattern. *A. K. Pope*

Looking south towards the crossing in March 1956 with only the empty trackbed of the Parkend Royal branch disappearing behnd the signal box. Parkend stone works on the left was once served by a siding off the Royal branch. As stated in chapter 3, the Midland's responsibility for the maintenance of permanent way, telegraphs, signalling, etc. extended north to a point just 6 chains short of Coleford Junction. The MR bracket signal illustrated was the northernmost of that company's origin, the remainder of the line to Cinderford, Coleford and Lydbrook, including the Mineral Loop, retaining GWR signals and equipment. Despite the longevity of some wooden posts, there are few photographs of the original GWR signals south of Coleford Junction, although these can be deduced from the pre-1906 diagrams. *E. Parker*

Another view of the remains of the stone works on 30th April 1962.   *R. Dagley-Morris*

buying. They soon discovered that they were paying rent on quarries which had not been worked for many years. It would also appear that Payne had concentrated his operations at Point Quarry, as the siding connection to the by then disused Parkend works was removed by the Joint Committee in April 1911 'after a long period of disuse'. United Stone Firms evidently planned, initially at least, to revive their new asset as, in January 1912, they applied to have the connection restored. However, by July of that year the application was withdrawn.

Just north of Payne's works, on the 'up' side of the main line, stood the Parkend Stone Works, established in 1889 by David & Company. This was served by a siding off the start of the Parkend Royal branch, and stood on the site of the old Brookhall Ditches loading bank. David & Company also owned fifteen quarries in the area. The machinery at the works included six horizontal sand and water saw

frames, three planing and moulding machines, one circular rubbing table, several lathes and an overhead gantry. Sixty masons were employed and the works were in operation night and day. In 1892 an amalgamation took place between several local quarry owners to form David & Sant Limited, further quarries being acquired until, in 1899, the group owned a total of forty-one. In 1900 David & Sant were taken over by the Forest of Dean Stone Firms Limited.

The United Stone Firms Company Limited was formed in 1910 and took over the majority of the stone enterprises in Dean including, as has been seen, Payne's. They also took over the Forest of Dean Stone Firms, but went into liquidation in 1917. The company, however, continued trading under the receiver until 1926, when Walter Bryant formed United Stone Firms (1926) Limited. In the next few years the new firm overcame many difficulties, but also went into liquidation in 1932 and Parkend Stone Works closed.

The stone works buildings in the 1930s. The signboard on the end of the left hand building reads 'Forest of Dean Stone Firms. Parkend Stone Works'.   *Mrs. D. Pope*

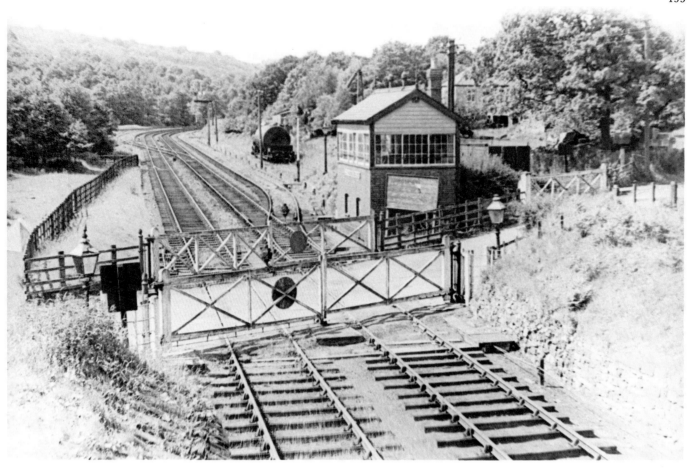

Looking north over the crossing into Coleford Junction on 22nd June 1947. The remainder of the line and associated industries from Coleford Junction to Cinderford inclusive is covered in the second volume.   *L. E. Copeland*

After leaving Parkend . . . .

    'then and then only are we well within the depth and mystery of the great woods. Oak, fern and foxglove border closely on the little line, the many curves of which, if the truth is to be told, are somewhat apt to unseat passengers too much engrossed with the fair scene through which they pass.'

A. O. Cooke
1913

ORIGINAL WILLIAM EASSIE STATION BUILDING

SCALE – 4 mm to 1 foot

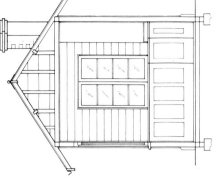

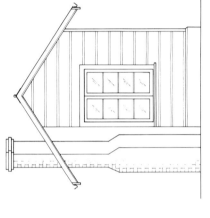

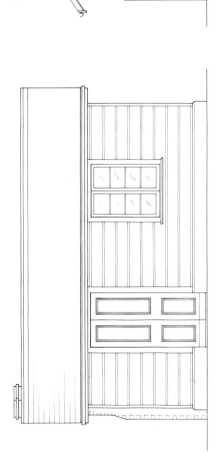

CROSS SECTION

END ELEVATION

ELEVATION TO PLATFORM

PLAN

W.C. FOR STATION

SCALE – 2 mm to 1 foot

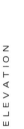
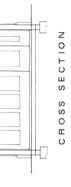

Believed to be the standard design for all the original 1875 William Eassie built S & W station buildings. The original drawing was prepared from measurements taken from existing Eassie buildings at Awre and Oakle Street.

This drawing was prepared from the original and all major dimensions are believed to be accurate, although some detail differences may have occurred as built. However, the internal measurement across the main structural members is drawn to 8′ 7½″ as scaled from the original drawing, not 8′ 6″ as specified.

N.B. The chimney could not have been constructed as drawn.

Bob How

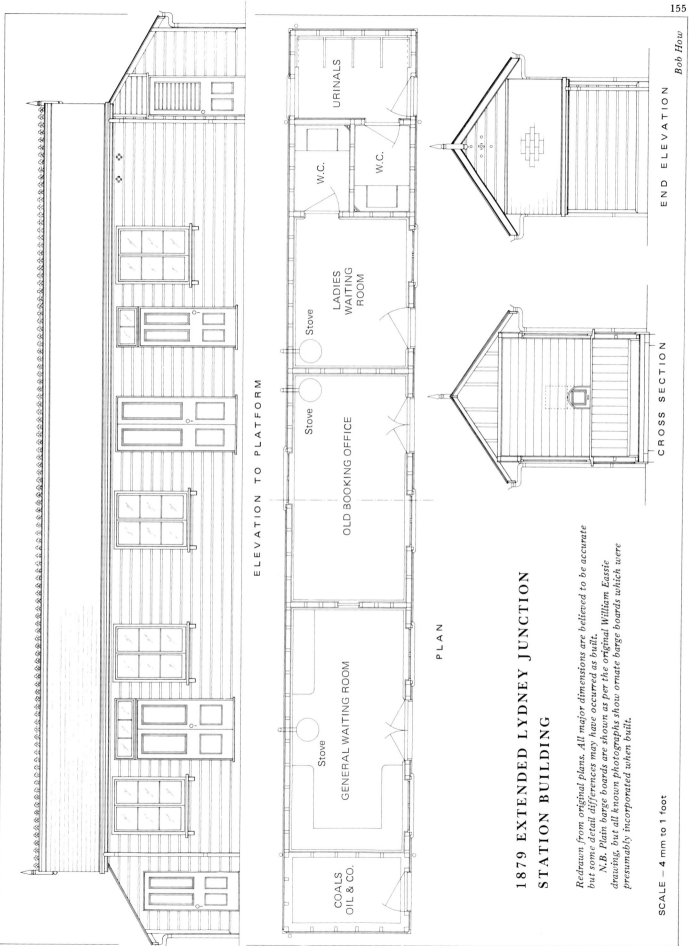

URINALS

W.C.

W.C.

LADIES
WAITING
ROOM

Stove

Stove

OLD BOOKING OFFICE

Stove

GENERAL WAITING ROOM

COALS
OIL & CO.

ELEVATION TO PLATFORM

END ELEVATION

Bob How

CROSS SECTION

PLAN

1879 EXTENDED LYDNEY JUNCTION
STATION BUILDING

*Redrawn from original plans. All major dimensions are believed to be accurate
but some detail differences may have occurred as built.
N.B. Plain barge boards are shown as per the original William Eassie
drawing, but all known photographs show ornate barge boards which were
presumably incorporated when built.*

SCALE – 4 mm to 1 foot

Bob How

1879 LYDNEY JUNCTION WAITING SHELTER

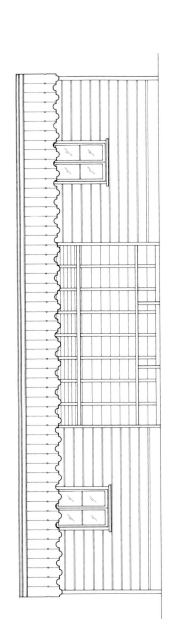

ELEVATION TO PLATFORM

END ELEVATION

PLAN

Based on original plans, but modified in detail to correspond with photographs.

SCALE – **4** mm to 1 foot

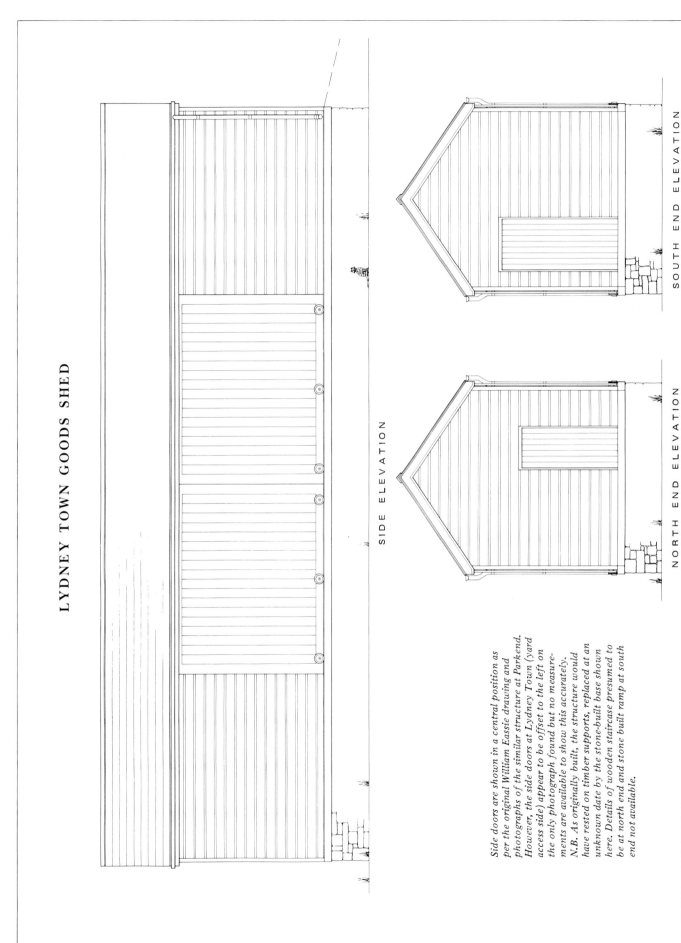

LYDNEY TOWN GOODS SHED

SIDE ELEVATION

NORTH END ELEVATION

SOUTH END ELEVATION

Bob How

Side doors are shown in a central position as per the original William Eassie drawing and photographs of the similar structure at Parkend. However, the side doors at Lydney Town (yard access side) appear to be offset to the left on the only photograph found but no measurements are available to show this accurately. N.B. As originally built, the structure would have rested on timber supports, replaced at an unknown date by the stone-built base shown here. Details of wooden staircase presumed to be at north end and stone built ramp at south end not available.

SCALE – 4 mm to 1 foot

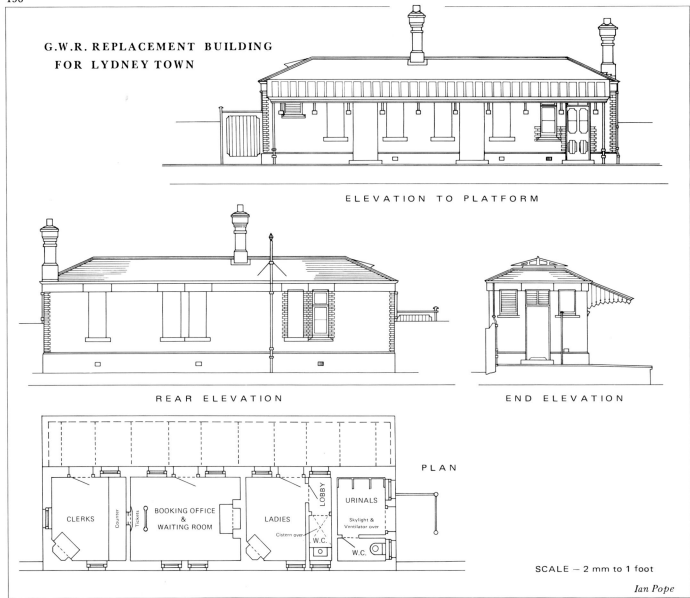

G.W.R. REPLACEMENT BUILDING
FOR LYDNEY TOWN

ELEVATION TO PLATFORM

REAR ELEVATION

END ELEVATION

PLAN

CLERKS

Counter

Tickets

BOOKING OFFICE
&
WAITING ROOM

LADIES

Cistern over

LOBBY

W.C.

URINALS

Skylight &
Ventilator over

W.C.

SCALE — 2 mm to 1 foot

Ian Pope

ACKNOWLEDGEMENTS

The compilation of this book has enabled the three of us to discover and, to a certain extent, share precious knowledge of the unique railway system that once served the Forest of Dean. For Ian, with his boyhood memories (and photographs) of footplate trips on the Lydney pannier tanks, it has been a nostalgic experience, but Bob and I were drawn to the area by its sheer fascination, inspired and guided by Harry Paar's pioneering work. We have all been particularly fortunate, not only in enlisting the co-operation of the former 'Dean Forester' team, but also in receiving their active support and enthusiasm. Peter Copeland's photographic surveys have provided the backbone for much of our research for he had the foresight to cycle to the Forest from Cheltenham on Sundays to photograph much of the system. We all owe him much gratitude for allowing us sight of the railway, much of which would surely have otherwise passed unrecorded. He also managed to save much vital official paperwork including signalling diagrams. Rev. David Tipper kindly allowed us free access to his valuable collection, which includes, for instance, notes of interviews with the late Inspector Bracey, and Harry Paar also received us warmly and offered much valuable help and advice. With such support we certainly had a lot to try and live up to!

As is so often the case with research, we find ourselves at the head of a large team, each member of which has made a vital contribution. Roger Carpenter introduced us to Peter Copeland in the first place and is therefore mainly responsible for getting things going. He also spent many hours printing up Peter's negatives. Alec Pope, Ian's father, was incredibly generous, not least in hospitality, as we systematically picked his brains and raided his cupboards. Keith Waters has copied and skilfully revived an embarrassing number of old photographs with results well beyond our most optimistic expectations and Tony Smith has spent many hours printing a wide range of negatives. Neil Parkhouse has been particularly generous in allowing us free access to his extensive and valuable collection of Forest postcards, many of which provide unique information. We are also privileged to have met former S & W Joint Committee signalman, Hedley Woodward, and drivers Cliff Wintle and Jim Imm, through whom we have gained much valuable knowledge of operation etc. In fact we spent two whole days with Jim going over many details and listening to his memories.

We should also like to thank Aerofilms, P. Ball, B. Baxter, G. Beale, W. A. Camwell, Central Electricity Generating Board, R. & J. Dagley-Morris, T. J. Edgington, Fred Elton, Gloucester Railway Carriage & Wagon Company, E. Gwynne, J. T. Howard Turner, Mrs. Knight, Lens of Sutton, John Mann, Bob Marrows, Eric Parker, Bill Potter, John Powell, T. Radway, Mike Rees, J. Rodway, John Stengelhofen, D. Thompson, V. R. Webster, Kelvin White, and Mike Christensen who caused havoc when checking our signalling details at the eleventh hour. He has foolishly agreed to write a signalling chapter in a subsequent volume.

Thanks also to David & Charles for permitting the use of the L & GRP photographs; British Rail, particularly Mr. Hajwa; and the Public Record Office at Kew. Finally Clare, Chris and June for typing, retyping and checking the manuscript and much appreciated moral support.